The
NATIONAL PARKS
and Other Wild Places of
MALAYSIA

The
NATIONAL PARKS
and Other Wild Places of
MALAYSIA

Text by WWF Malaysia
Photographs by Gerald Cubitt

Produced in association with
the World Wide Fund For Nature Malaysia

NH
NEW
HOLLAND

First published in 1998 by New Holland Publishers (UK) Ltd
London • Cape Town • Sydney • Singapore

2 4 6 8 10 9 7 5 3 1

24 Nutford Place, London W1H 6DQ, United Kingdom

80 Mckenzie Street, Cape Town 8001, South Africa

Level 1/Unit 4, 14 Aquatic Drive, Frenchs Forest, NSW 2086, Australia

ISBN 1 85368 626 3

Project Director: Charlotte Parry-Crooke   Cartography: William Smuts
Editors: Richard Hammond, Ann Baggaley   Index: Janet Dudley
Editorial assistance: Rowena Curtis   Additional styling: Roger Daniels,
Designer: Alan Marshall   Grahame Dudley, Behram Kapadia

Reproduction by Pica Colour Separation
Overseas (Pte) Ltd, Singapore
Printed and bound in Malaysia by Times Offset (M) Sdn Bhd

Publishers' Note

Throughout this book species are, where possible, referred to by their common as opposed to scientific names for ease of reference by the general reader. Where no common names exist, scientific names are used. Many of the titles listed in the further reading section on page 174 provide full scientific names for species found in Malaysia. The maps contained in the book are intended as 'locators' only; detailed, large-scale maps should be consulted when planning a trip. It is important to note that access, accommodation and other details vary as new transport methods and facilities develop. Remember that trail routes can vary, river courses can change, and water depths can alter dramatically within minutes. Although the publishers and WWF Malaysia have made every effort to ensure that the information contained in this book was correct at the time of going to press, they accept no responsibility for any loss, injury or inconvenience sustained by any person using the book.

GLOSSARY

The Malay words listed below commonly occur in placenames and many of them are used in this book.

Air panas	Hot springs	Lubuk	Deep pool
Air terjun	Waterfall	Muara	River mouth,
Ampang,	Dam		estuary
Ampangan		Negara	Country/national
Batang	Large river	Negeri	State
Batu	Rock, stone	Padang	Open space
Bukit	Hill	Pantai	Beach
Bumbun	Hide	Pelabuhan	Port, harbour
Dusun	Orchard	Pengkalan	Jetty
Genting	Mountain pass	Pulau	Island
Gua	Cave	Rantau	Straight coastline
Gunung	Mountain	Rimba	Jungle
Hilir	Lower reaches of	Rumah rehat	Resthouse
	river	Seberang	Far bank of river
Hutan	Jungle, forest	Selat	Strait
Jambatan	Bridge	Semenanjung	Peninsula
Jeram	Rapids	Sungai	River
Kampung	Village	Taman	Park
Kerangas	Heath-forest	Tanah	Land
Kota	Fort or city	Tanjung	Headland, cape
Kuala	River mouth,	Tasik	Lake
	confluence	Telaga	Spring, well
Labuhan	Port	Teluk	Bay
Laut	Sea	Ujung	Cape
Loagan	Lake (in Sarawak)	Ulu	Upriver

Map legend for section maps shown between pages 23 and 168

———————	Main road
———————	Secondary road
- - - - - - -	Track
----------------	Railway
BRUNEI	International boundary
- - - - - - -	State boundary
- - - - - - -	Protected Area boundary
Kuala Lumpur ○	City or major town
Seremban ○	Village or small town
Park HQ ▢	General information
Four Steps Waterfall ●	Place of interest
S.Teku	Water feature
Gn.Rabung 2187m ▲ (7186ft)	Peak in metres (feet)
✈	Airport
Laban Rata hut ⛫	Hut site
Melinau Camp ▲	Camp site
Ubah shelter ⊓	Shelter

CONTENTS

ACKNOWLEDGEMENTS

CONTRIBUTORS
The text for this book was prepared by the staff of the World Wide Fund For Nature Malaysia, including the following:

Amlir Ayat • Balu Perumal • Daria Mathew • Dr Dionysius Sharma • Dr Geoffrey Davison
Hymeir Kamarudin • Dr Isabelle Louis • Dr Junaidi Payne • Justine Vaz • Khoo Ming Ghee
Lim Li Ching • Dato' Dr Mikaail Kavanagh Abdullah • Muhamad Nasir Abdul Salam
Pamela Fletcher • Dr Rajanathan Rajaratnam • Reza Azmi • Shahril Kamarulzaman

PHOTOGRAPHER'S ACKNOWLEDGEMENTS
In addition to those acknowledged on page 9, the principal photographer gratefully acknowledges the generous support of the following during his travels in Malaysia:

Hotel Istana, Kuala Lumpur • Taman Negara Resort, Pahang • Holiday Inn, Kuching
Holiday Inn, Miri • Promenade Hotel, Kota Kinabalu

Peninsular Malaysia: Berjaya Redang Beach Resort, Pulau Redang • The Datai, Langkawi • Fully Inn,
Gua Musang • Golden Sands Hotel, Penang • Jelai Highlands Resort, Fraser's Hill • Perdana Stong Hill Resort,
Kelantan • Rumau Rehat, Kuala Lipis • Sutra Beach Resort, Terengganu

Sarawak: Batang Ai Longhouse Resort • Plaza Hotel, Bintulu • Royal Mulu Resort

Sabah: Borneo Rainforest Lodge, Danum Valley • Executive Hotel, Lahad Datu • Gunung Emas
Highlands Resort • Sukau Rainforest Lodge

SPECIAL PHOTOGRAPHER'S ACKNOWLEDGEMENT
The principal photographer wishes to extend his great debt of gratitude to his wife, Janet, who accompanied him throughout his travels in Malaysia, providing not only practical support but also insight and perception into every aspect of his photography.

PHOTOGRAPHIC ACKNOWLEDGEMENTS
The World Wide Fund For Nature Malaysia, the publishers and the principal photographer extend their thanks to the following who generously loaned their photographs for inclusion in this book. With the exception of those listed below, all the photographs in the book were taken by Gerald Cubitt.

Michael Aw (*Ocean N Environment*): p166 (tl; r); p168 (b); p169 (both subjects) • *Chan Chew Lun* (*Natural History Publications*): p17 (r) • *Tommy Chang* (*Tommy Chang Image Productions*): p132 (tr) • *Chew Yen Fook*: p38 (tr); p48 (bl); p144 (cl); p146 (tr) • *Linda Dunk*: p78 (tl); p166 (cl) *Martin Edge*: p26 (r); p57 (r); p80 (cl); p134 (t); p135 (r); p167; p168 (tl) • *Footprints*: p140; (*Philip Waldock*): pp128–9 *Jill Gocher*: p93 (cr); p96 (bl); 98 (tl); p99 (b); p102 (both subjects); p106 (tl; bl); p113 (c); p116 (bl); p118; p119; p120 (bc) *Christopher Gow* (*Symbiosis Expedition Planning*): pp4–5; p120 (tr); • *Martin Harvey*: p13; p31; p34 (tl); p154 (tl) *Jack Jackson*: p26 (bl); p55; p78 (bl; r); p81 (r); p105 (b); p135 (tl); p153 (tr); p166 (bl) • *A. Lamb*: p120 (tl); p126 (c); p132 (b); p138 (bl) • *Life File* (*Emma Lee*): pp56–7 *Malaysian Tourism Promotion Board*: p68 (cl); p100 (bl) *Oceanic Impressions* (*Mark Strickland*): p26 (tl; cl); p29 (tl; cr); p56 (tl; cl); p80 (tl; bl); p133; p153 (cr) • *Photobank* (*Singapore: Tettoni, Cassio and Associates*): p25 (t); pp82–3 • *Linda Pitkin*: p76 (bl); p142 (bl) • *Craig Potton* (*Craig Potton Publishing*): p144 (r) • *Jesus Cede Prudente* (*Wildlife Expeditions*): pp6–7; p40 (tl; bl); p43 (br); p44 (r); p60 (tl); p104 (b); p105 (tr); p107; p115; p117 (r); p154 (bl); pp158–9; p159 (tl; tr); p162 (tr) *Raleigh International*: p68 (tl); (*Ian Robinson*): p108 (t)

Radin Mohd Noh Saleh: p37 • *Sarawak Tourist Board*: p89 (cr); p98 (bl); p127 (br) • *Morten Strange* (*Flying Colours Photography*): p43 (tr; cr); p46 (c); p103; p163; p164 (tr; br) • *Struik Image Library* (*Andrew Bannister*): p17 (l; c); p92 (l); pp92–3 *Wayne Tarman* (*Travelcom Asia*): p87; pp88–9; p94 (cl); p96 (r); p104–5; p121 (r) • *Arthur Teng*: p68 (bl); pp100–1; pp142–3; p148–9 • *Albert Teo* (*Borneo Eco Tours*): p88 (l); p97; p110; p127 (t); pp138–9; p139 (cr; br); pp152–3; p153 (br); p159 (br) • *Tham Yau Kong* (*Borneo Endeavour*): p130 (r); p131; p132 (tl); p139 (tr); p148 (bl) • *Henrietta Van den Bergh*: p16 (c); p24 (b); p25 (b); p27; pp28–9; p29 (tr); p32 (tl); p34 (bl; c); pp34–5; p40 (r); p44 (bl); p58 (cl); p60 (tr); p61; p62 (bl; br); p86 (tl); p157; p160 (tl; bl; br); p162 (bl) • *Wilderness Photography* (*Jerry Wooldridge*): p120 (bl); p121 (l); p124 (r) • *Windrush Photos* (*Arnoud B. Van den Berg*): p45 • *Lawson Wood*: p15 (r); p28 (l); p56 (bl); p129 (r); p141; p142 (tl); p143 (br); p150; p151 • *World Wide Fund For Nature Malaysia* (*Azwad M. N.*): p79; (*Yusof Ghani*): p49; (*S. H. Lim*): pp52–3; (*Elley Lina*): p89 (tr; br); (*A. Maslennikov*): p48 (br); (*Muhamad Nasir*): p73 (br); (*Jesus Cede Prudente*): pp122–3

t = top; b = bottom; c = centre; l = left; r = right

Illustrations appearing in the preliminary pages are as follows:
Half-title: Silvered Leaf-monkey and baby; Title pages: Pulau Tiga, Sabah; Pages 4–5: River transport at Ulu Ai, Sarawak; Pages 6–7: Oriental Pied Hornbill; Pages 8–9: Coconut palms at Setiu, Terengganu; Pages 10–11: Sunset at Tanjung Aru, Sabah.

ACKNOWLEDGEMENTS

The World Wide Fund For Nature Malaysia, the publishers and the principal photographer wish to express their gratitude to the following for their generous and valuable assistance during the preparation of this book:

Dato' Sabbaruddin Chik, Minister of Culture, Arts and Tourism, Malaysia

Tan Sri Dato' Paduka Khir Johari, President, World Wide Fund For Nature Malaysia

Ministry of Culture, Arts and Tourism, Malaysia • Malaysia Tourism Promotion Board (Tourism Malaysia), Kuala Lumpur and London • Sarawak Ministry of Tourism • Sarawak Tourism Board Sabah Ministry of Tourism and Environmental Development • Sabah Tourism Promotion Corporation

Department of Wildlife and National Parks • Musa Nordin, Director General of Wildlife and National Parks • Department of Fisheries • Sarawak Forest Department, especially the National Parks and Wildlife Office • Sapuan bin Ahmad, Forest Department, Sarawak • Sabah Forest Department Sabah Parks • Sabah Wildlife Department • Francis Liew, Sabah Parks

The officers, staff and guides of all the parks and reserves visited during the preparation of this book, and the photography for it, and for all assistance previously provided to WWF Malaysia

Asian Overland Services, Kuala Lumpur • Emasewa Sdn. Bhd. National Car Rental • Jean-Fernand Wasser (formerly General Manager, Istana Hotel, Kuala Lumpur and now Area Director of SMI Resorts)

PENINSULAR MALAYSIA
Cindy L.C. Lim and Mohd. Salehuddin Zainuddin, International Marketing, Malaysian Tourism Promotion Board • Susan Abraham • Mark Anderson • Hazie Aris-Rafflee • Asian Overland Services: Anthony Wong and Mark Suppiah • Zain Sharer Awin • Othman Ayeb • Hafina Abu Bakar • Albert Chen • Joe Chong Fraser's Hill Development Corporation • David Goh, Penang Butterfly Farm • Mavis Hedrik • Mike Wong Wai Hong • K. Kaliyannan • Hymeir Kamarudin • Mitchell Kelly • The staff of the Kuala Lipis Tourist Office Langkawi Coral • Dr Kevin Lazarus, Taiping Zoo • Foo Siew Lin • Malaysian Nature Society, including the staff of the society and of the Kuala Selangor Nature Park • Narelle McMurtrie • Robyn Marais • Hashim bin Man • Irshad Mobarak • En. Nasaruddin • Tumah Said • Mohd. Hanan Samsi • Mohd. Samsuddin b. Mohd. Suri • Ken Scriven • Weuta Ah Rom Yazid Mohamed, Ministry of Culture, Arts and Tourism, Malaysia • Sulaiman Yahya, Renong Berhad • Peter Yeo • Masood Yusof • Zamiza Zainal • En. Zulkisli

SARAWAK
Robert Basiuk, Sarawak Tourism Board • Adrian Cornelius • David Gibbs • Jong's Crocodile Farm Fiona Kho • Walter J. Kohli • Nicholas Leong • Winston Anthony Marshall • Taman Tumbina Bintulu Wayne Tarman, Travelcom Asia • Darrell Tsen • James Wan • Christina Wendt • Joseph C.F. Wong Philip Yong, Borneo Adventure

SABAH
Irene Benggon Chararuks, Nuredah Othman and Normegaurati bte. Sapian, Sabah Tourism Promotion Corporation • Wendy Hutton • Harry Lohok • Tulip Noorazyze • Nurul S. Abdullah • Dr Junaidi Payne Jesus Cede Prudente, Wildlife Expeditions • Homathevi Raaman • Abd. Sail Hj. Jamaludin • Bulangai Sandor • Dr Waidi Sinun • Tanjung Aru Tours and Travel • Albert Teo, Borneo Eco Tours • Tham Yau Kong, Borneo Endeavour • Yayasan Sabah, Tourism and Leisure Division

SINGAPORE
Bernard Harrison, Singapore Zoological Gardens and Night Safari • Amanda Chew • Vasantha Nugegoda

GREAT BRITAIN
Sharon Balding • Dr Richard Bonser, University of Manchester • Colonel John Eliot • DDFE Resources • Christopher Gow, Symbiosis Expedition Planning • Robert Hodgkinson • Jack Jackson Malaysian Tourism Promotion Board (Tourism Malaysia), London: Amran Rahman • Natural History Museum, London: Dr Jeremy Holloway • Fiona Nichols • Helen Oon, Sarawak Tourism Liaison • Raleigh International • Ian Robinson • Royal Botanic Gardens, Kew: Dr John Dransfield, Jill Cowley, Dr David Pegler, Jeffrey Wood • Royal Botanic Garden, Edinburgh: Professor Roy Watling, David Mitchell Henrietta Van den Bergh, Prospero Productions • Dr David Wells

SPECIAL PUBLISHERS' ACKNOWLEDGEMENT
The publishers would like to express their special thanks to Dato' Dr Mikaail Kavanagh Abdullah and all the staff of WWF Malaysia including not only the contributors but also all the staff who made this project possible. A special debt of gratitude is due to Dr G.W.H. Davison for co-ordinating the project and for seeing it through to fruition.

منتري كبودايأن كسنيان دان ڤلنچوڠن مليسيا

MENTERI KEBUDAYAAN, KESENIAN DAN PELANCONGAN MALAYSIA

PREFACE

Malaysia's natural heritage is a source of great pride to the people of this country and over the centuries has fascinated naturalists, explorers and travellers from many other parts of the world. Today, thousands of visitors and holidaymakers come to Malaysia each year to share our delight in the land's diverse habitats and wildlife. The crown jewels of this rich treasurehouse are the country's protected areas – our national and state parks, wildlife reserves and sanctuaries.

We must not forget that these beautiful places are not only vital in ecological terms but also an important source of income both for the country as a whole and for local communities. It is estimated that by the year 2000 at least ten per cent of Malaysia's income will be derived from ecotourism-based activities.

Recognizing that the development of ecotourism depends upon a continuing programme of conservation, the Ministry of Culture, Arts and Tourism, Malaysia has taken steps to ensure that our unspoilt wild areas are utilized in ways that will preserve their natural and cultural value. With the assistance of the World Wide Fund For Nature Malaysia, the Ministry has prepared a National Ecotourism Plan to provide development guidelines and conservation measures needed for our forests, islands, highlands, wetlands, caves and beaches.

The Malaysian Government is committed to ensuring that such areas remain pristine and rich in diversity of life. I hope that this book will make both Malaysians and visitors aware of what a wonderful gift nature has bestowed upon us and realize why it is so important that we all work towards protecting it for the future.

Thank you.

Dato' Sabbaruddin Chik
Minister of Culture, Arts and Tourism, Malaysia

FOREWORD

WWF Malaysia has spent more than 25 years working hand-in-hand with our many partners in conservation in helping to conserve the beautiful wild places Malaysia is blessed with. The efforts of all – the government, private sector, universities, individuals and environmental organisations – have given us the many parks, wildlife sanctuaries and other protected areas that we have today.

This book is a celebration of these efforts and a tribute to what can be achieved if all parties who care for our natural heritage work together.

We face many challenges in the future. But I sincerely hope that we will still, in years to come, be able to enjoy those wild natural places, like the highlands, lowland forests, mangroves and reefs, which are, today, still pristine and unpolluted.

Tan Sri Dato' Paduka Khir Johari
President, WWF Malaysia

INTRODUCTION

Malaysia lies at the crossroads of Southeast Asia, readily accessible from almost anywhere in the world. This is a land of infinite diversity, in its culture and traditions and, perhaps above all, in its natural heritage, from ocean depths to mountain peaks.

Visitors to this beautiful country will experience nature on a grand scale – green rolling hills, granite peaks, vast expanses of ancient rain forest and everywhere rivers in all sizes and moods. Gibbons sing in the treetops, the shadowy bulk of an elephant may be glimpsed close by a trail and an astonishingly rich birdlife fills the forest with sights and sounds. This is where you will find the world's largest flower, rare orchids and a huge variety of palms. Offshore in the warm seas, coral reefs round rugged little islands teem with tropical fish and colourful marine life of all kinds – a paradise for divers and snorkellers.

A widespread system of parks and other conservation areas, linked to a wise policy of eco-tourism, ensures that both wildlife and habitats not only have the best chance of survival but can be seen and appreciated with the minimum of disturbance. Malaysia's tropical climate and nationwide travel network make it possible to visit many of these wonderful places all year round and to enjoy the outdoor pursuits that they offer, in perfect tranquillity far from the cities or crowded beaches.

At the Heart of Southeast Asia

Peninsular Malaysia hangs like a pendant from the southern tip of mainland Asia. The eleven states here, of which eight are hereditary sultanates, all have a coastline and most are based on a major river system of the same name:

The diverse habitats of the Malaysian rain forest (left) harbour over 240 species of mammals, including the Proboscis Monkey (above).

for example, the Sungai Kelantan, Sungai Terengganu, Sungai Perak and Sungai Pahang. More than 600 kilometres (400 miles) away to the east, across the South China Sea, lie the two remaining states, Sarawak and Sabah, occupying the northern third of the island of Borneo and together making up 60 per cent of the land area of the country.

The capital, Kuala Lumpur, is one of several big cities on the western coastal plain of the Peninsula, the most heavily populated part of the country. Each of the states also has its own capital town or city; in the Borneo states, Kuching is the capital of Sarawak and Kota Kinabalu the capital of Sabah.

Malaysia's population is extremely diverse, a little more than half consisting of Malays, with large minority groups of Chinese and Indian origin, and many different groups of indigenous people. One of the country's great attractions is the harmony in which this variety of peoples co-exist and the delight they take in one another's company. Many people routinely speak three or four languages, although the national language, Bahasa Malaysia, is the most widely spoken. Foreign visitors can usually get by comfortably with English, even in remote areas.

Malaysia's Biogeographical Development

Geographically and biologically, Peninsular Malaysia, Sarawak and Sabah are part of the Sunda Shelf, a small tectonic plate abutting mainland Asia on the one side and the Australasian (Sahul) Shelf on the other. In the Miocene period, about 15 million years ago, a large drop in sea level linked all of the Malay Peninsula (so-named in geographical terms), Sumatra, Borneo and Java in one single landmass. Smaller fluctuations occurred during subsequent periods, although there is geographical evidence that shows that the sea level was never more than about five metres (16 feet) above that of the present day.

Continual joining and separation of these major islands and peninsulas has been responsible for many of their similarities and differences. The faunal and floral groups of the Malay Peninsula, Sumatra, Borneo and Java are all more similar to one another than any one of them is to the land beyond, for example mainland Asia. Yet each has unique species, with very limited distributions.

Individual anomalies, such as the survival of the Orang-utan in Borneo and Sumatra, but not in Java or the Malay Peninsula; the occurrence of the Green Peafowl in the Peninsula and Java; the presence of the Agile Gibbon in three isolated and distinct populations in limited segments of the Peninsula, Sumatra and Borneo, where they are surrounded by populations of other species; each of these can usually be explained individually in terms of historical geography. Yet, together, the thousands of different plant and animal distributions present a stunning image of how the biological world must have shifted and flowed through time and space, in complex and sometimes contradictory ways. This historical aspect to biological diversity is overlain by a great range of differences in habitats that depend on rainfall, slope, soil and rock types, altitude, drainage and other environmental features which determine what species occur in any given area.

Natural Riches and Diversity

When asked how many plants and animals occur in Malaysia, it is impossible to give a satisfactory answer. For certain groups, such as birds, the numbers of species are known quite precisely, and for other groups, such as trees, the numbers in Peninsular Malaysia are reasonably well known, but the state of knowledge in other parts of the country is less complete. In many groups the degree of overlap or difference between the species that occur in the Peninsula and in the Bornean territories of Sarawak and Sabah has not been investigated in detail.

It is certain, however, that Malaysia is one of the twelve most biologically diverse countries in the world. For example, there are about 1,200 species of orchids in Kinabalu Park. There are 637 species of birds known from Peninsular Malaysia, of which nearly three-quarters are resident, a much higher total than in temperate countries. There are more than 1,160 species of ferns in the whole country. Mammals include 216 species in the Peninsula and 218 in Sabah and Sarawak, the latter total including 40 species that are endemic to Borneo.

To protect a wide and representative range of the species, one reserve is not enough. It is necessary to have a network of protected areas, some large and some small, selected carefully for the species and habitats they contain, and for the practicability of management.

Conserving the Natural Heritage

Malaysia has had a long and active involvement in conservation. The first forest reserves were set up in the 19th century and the first wildlife reserve, Chior in Perak (now no longer operative), in 1902. Taman Negara, the country's first national park, was gazetted in 1938–39 and from then until today the process of setting aside land for protection has continued, with new areas continually being proposed.

The protection and management of land and sea areas is a complex undertaking. Generally speaking, nearly all forested land is owned and managed by government. Some of it is on state land, but the majority is contained within forest reserves that are managed by the respective Forestry Departments in the Peninsula, Sarawak and Sabah.

In Peninsular Malaysia, forest reserves are either productive (for the selective extraction of such resources as timber, rattan and bamboo) or protective (for conservation). Under other more detailed categories, forest reserves may be classified for research, education, soil protection, water catchment areas and various other purposes. Wildlife is under the protection and management of the Department of Wildlife and National Parks. At sea, marine parks, turtles and marine mammals are the responsibility of the Department of Fisheries.

In Sarawak, the wildlife and forestry authorities are combined. The system of forest reserves is similar to that in the Peninsula, but there are three categories: commercial, communal and protected. The National Parks and Wildlife Office, within the Sarawak Forest Department, manages the national parks, wildlife sanctuaries and cen-

tres, and nature reserves. Under the same system, progress has been made in constituting certain islands as marine parks. Most categories of conservation areas are open to the public but wildlife sanctuaries – such as Lanjak-Entimau – are for strict protection.

Sabah's system of forest reserves under the Sabah Forest Department is classified into seven categories, which include protection forest, such as the crucial Danum Valley Conservation Area, and wildlife reserves. The management of the latter is in the hands of the Sabah Wildlife Department, and that of parks, including some island and sea areas, comes under the jurisdiction of Sabah Parks.

Of the many non-governmental organizations in Malaysia, several are devoted to conservation of nature and the environment. They try to work in a constructive and positive way, often in conjunction with government, helping with the identification of potential protected areas, habitat surveys, single species studies, and the production of educational materials. Among them, three of the more prominent which operate nationwide include the World Wide Fund For Nature (WWF) Malaysia, the Malaysian Nature Society and the Malaysian Society of Marine Sciences. The first two have full-time scientific staff, but all may also from time to time welcome the assistance of volunteers in conservation projects. An initial enquiry (see Useful Addresses, p.174) should yield information on current opportunities.

Conservation Today

In Peninsular Malaysia, almost half of the land area is covered by natural tropical evergreen rain forest. Most of this is within forest reserves and includes about 80 small plots – most are less than 10 square kilometres (4 square miles) – which are called Virgin Jungle Reserves, meant as samples of untouched forest, as well as Protection Forest that lies mainly on high, steep ground. In addition, there are 15 protected areas of land and inland waters, of varying status, that total 6,899 square kilometres (2,664 square miles). The four biggest are Taman Negara (4,343 square kilometres/1,677 square miles), Endau Rompin (the two sectors of which total 789 square kilometres/305 square miles), Cameron Highlands Wildlife Sanctuary (649 square kilome-

tres/250 square miles) and Krau Wildlife Reserve (530 square kilometres/205 square miles). There are 38 islands whose waters are protected as marine reserves, to a limit of approximately 3 kilometres (2 nautical miles) offshore.

Well over half of Sarawak's land area is covered by forest, much of which is either within, or has been committed for incorporation into, forest reserves. There are so far ten national parks, three wildlife sanctuaries and several nature reserves, totalling about 2,901 square kilometres (1,120 square miles). By far the biggest is Lanjak-Entimau Wildlife Sanctuary (1,688 square kilometres/652 square miles) which is adjacent to a still larger area in Kalimantan (Indonesia), the two protecting over 10,000 square kilometres (3,861 square miles).

Sabah's forests, too, cover over half of the state. Most of these are within forest reserves, with the remainder in parks and wildlife reserves. There are six parks, six wildlife reserves and bird sanctuaries, and several areas of other protected status, totalling about 5,270 square kilometres (2,035 square miles). By far the biggest areas are Crocker Range National Park at 1,399 square kilometres (540 square miles) and Tabin Wildlife Reserve at 1,205 square kilometres (465 square miles), but Kinabalu Park at 754 square kilometres (291 square miles) is geographically outstanding. Several of the parks include the sea area around islands. Offshore from Sabah, and now a federal territory administered from Kuala Lumpur, three little islands off Labuan have their waters protected as a marine park.

Visiting Malaysia's Protected Areas

This book covers the parks and other protected areas of major or specific interest that are generally open to the public. When planning a visit it is important first to contact the relevant authority (see page 174) for advice, as bookings may be necessary. Not all the sites that

From left to right: *Malaysia's terrain is enormously varied, ranging from sparkling beaches to rocky torrents, from the spectacular granite peaks of Gunung Kinabalu, highest mountain in Southeast Asia, to tropical islands such as Pulau Sipadan, internationally renowned as a top diving spot.*

are covered in this book are parks, because many other areas are important for wildlife and exciting to visit.

Many of the parks have accommodation, walking trails and basic amenities, and a number have good information centres. The visitor information panels given in the book for each area provide a brief resumé of what you can expect to find.

Most protected areas on land are forested, and it is wise for visitors to bring clothing that is light yet will give protection from thorns. Heavy-duty boots are seldom needed unless mountain climbing is included in your itinerary, but footwear should be tough enough to withstand wetting or ripping. Only a few parks can supply camping equipment, and in some camping is not normally permitted.

Large wild animals, scorpions or snakes are unlikely to be a threat to visitors – many people do not see a single snake, even when spending a week or two entirely in the forest. Nevertheless, due care is needed so as not to disturb animals that may prove dangerous. Smaller creatures such as mosquitoes are usually no more than a minor irritant and though leeches are difficult to exclude completely, they can be discouraged by an aerosol insect repellant. Less damaging to the environment, the juice from wetted tobacco, soap rubbed on boots, or a strong salt solution can all help to prevent a leech from biting, and can be applied directly to a leech in order to remove it.

Other sensible precautions include not eating plants or fruits with which you are unfamiliar (the strict rule in all places is never to pick any flowers or uproot plants), to take medical advice before a trip, especially if you are not familiar with the tropical environment, and, though serious diseases are seldom a problem for visitors to parks, to seek immediate treatment for any unusual symptom.

Malaysia's forests abound in wildlife and plantlife. Diverse botanical delights include gingers (below left) *and orchids* (below right); *elephants* (below centre) *are among the large mammals you may possibly encounter.*

Getting lost, or having an accident which prevents you from returning to camp, are small risks but ones which should be borne in mind. Travelling in a group, with a guide, staying on marked routes, and having proper equipment are all wise precautions.

The marine parks are the places where visitors may find the most need for specialized equipment. On some islands there are companies which may rent scuba diving gear to visitors, and which can provide guidance by dive masters. The less-visited parks have no such facilities and divers must take their own responsibility for ensuring that they are fully prepared and properly equipped.

Wildlife Watching and Botanizing

Although it can be hard work searching for animals in the tropical rain forest, the rewards are great. Learn to watch and listen, and above all to be still, and the green world around you will come alive.

Sightings of scarce and secretive animals such as tigers, leopards and rhinoceroses are rare, but spotting a footprint on the trail or in the soft mud of a wallow can be a thrill in itself. Remember to look up into the canopy, where leaf-monkeys, macaques and squirrels inhabit the upper branches. Some parks have canopy walkways, high above the forest floor, that give you a bird's-eye view of life in the treetops. At night, it is sometimes possible to go out on the trail with a spotlight or to wait in a hide by a saltlick or mud wallow where deer, wild pigs and possibly a tapir may visit on their nocturnal wanderings.

Malaysia's most famous mammal, the Orang-utan, is adept at keeping itself well hidden but visitors to the Orang-utan Rehabilitation Centre at Sepilok in Sabah, which prepares captive animals for a return to the wild, have an excellent chance of seeing this magnificent ape at close quarters. Other fascinating primates are the gibbons and it is worth going out into the forest very early in the morning to hear their 'dawn chorus'. Birds are generally easier to see than mammals, and Malaysia is one of the finest places in the world for birdwatching.

The coast is the place to watch marine turtles coming ashore to lay their eggs, and you should keep an eye open out to sea for the humped backs of porpoises breaking through the waves. Beneath the surface of Malaysia's warm turquoise waters are glorious submarine gardens of corals filled with tropical fish of all shapes and hues, sea fans, sponges and sea anemones. In some areas graceful reef sharks constantly patrol their territory – usually quite harmless to responsible divers who observe the code of safety.

Keen botanists can be assured of delights everywhere. The lowland forests are rich in tree species and here lush vegetation, enormous strangling figs twisted in labyrinthine coils and dangling lianas are the very essence of the 'jungle'. At higher zones, epiphytic orchids can be seen in the trees and in montane areas there are colourful rhododendrons.

Malaysia even has parks especially for the protection of individual plant species. In Sarawak, Kubah is one of the most important sites worldwide for palms, and at Gunung Gading the sight of a giant *Rafflesia* in bloom repays the patient watcher who waits for the bud to burst open and spread its huge petals for just a few brief days.

Visitor Activities

The visitor has an enormous choice of activities in Malaysia's parks, from the relaxing to the strenuous. It is not necessary to be at the peak of physical fitness – much quiet enjoyment can be gained just by strolling along a nature trail or bathing in a forest pool.

Some of the longer treks, however, can take several days to complete, with overnight camps along the way, and especially over hilly ground can be very demanding on the walker. Those attempting an ascent of one of Malaysia's challenging peaks can expect in places to be faced with a steep scramble where climbing experience would be both useful and desirable.

Aficionados of watersports are particularly well served. Inland, on the rivers, the truly intrepid can test their nerve with whitewater rafting or canoeing down rapids. On the coast or on one of the offshore islands, snorkellers and divers have a superb selection of prime dive sites to explore, and, at the more visited resorts, windsurfing and sailing are popular options.

Local Life

Many of Malaysia's protected areas are close to the homes of local communities, such as the Orang Hulu in Endau Rompin in the Peninsula, the Penan at Gunung Mulu, Sarawak and the Kadazan Dusun of Kinabalu in Sabah. Though largely adhering to their traditional lifestyles, and retaining their ancient rights to hunt for food and collect forest produce, today these people often play an active role not only in the conservation and sustainable management of the land but also, increasingly, in the development of tourism.

In some areas it is possible to arrange accommodation in traditional longhouses and to hire village boats and other transport. All guests must observe the communities' customs and etiquette, and respect their right to privacy at all times.

The Value of the Natural World

The presence of rich plant and animal communities is not the only reason why it is interesting to visit wild places. As well as the intellectual puzzle of understanding why the natural world is the way it is – and the forest or the tropical reef can give insights to us all – there are physical challenges to meet and a rare peace to savour. While enjoying all that Malaysia's parks have to offer, we can also learn at first hand how vital it is that such places should remain unspoilt by commercialism, and be preserved and protected as an irreplaceable treasure.

Traditional costumes are worn on special occasions by Sarawak's Iban (below left) *and Sabah's Rungus* (below right). *Even in the Peninsula, rural homes* (below centre) *often retain a traditional air.*

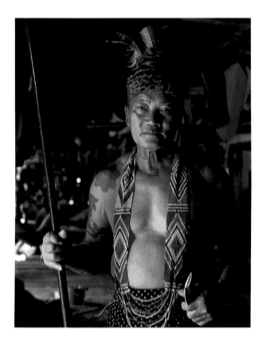

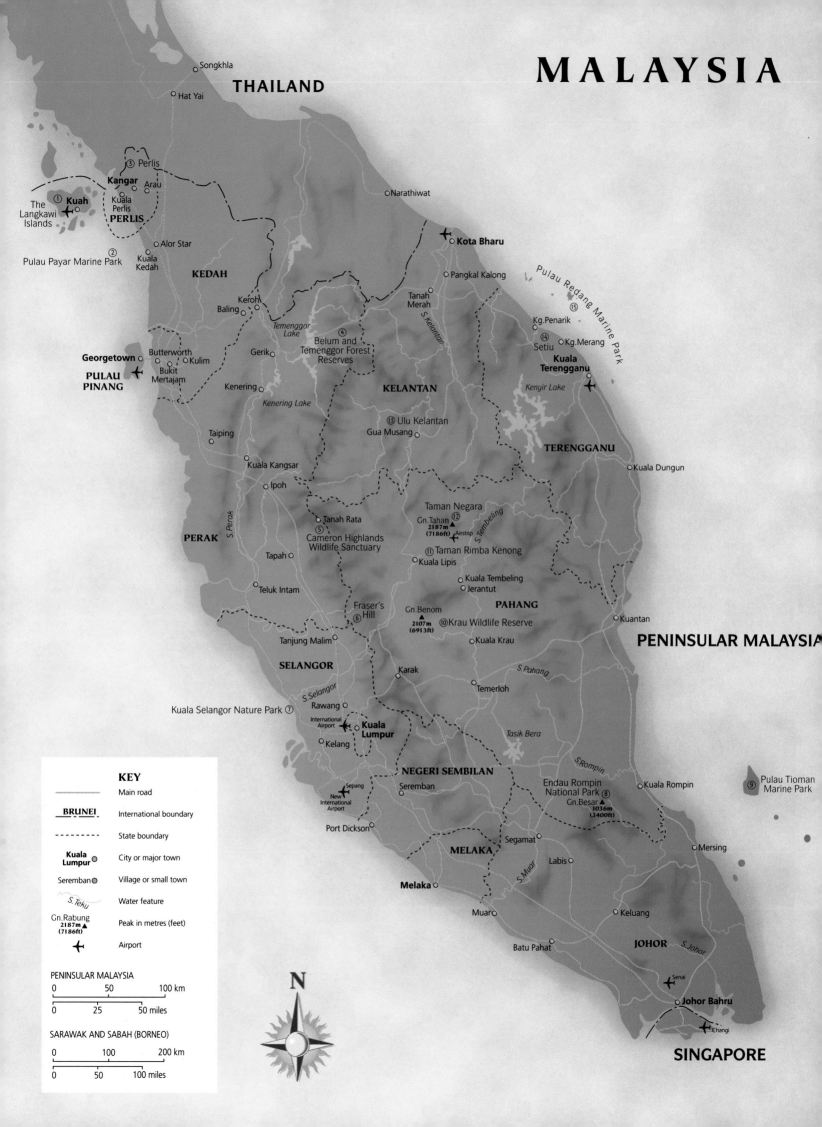

MALAYSIA

THAILAND

Songkhla
Hat Yai
Narathiwat

① Kuah
The Langkawi Islands
③ Perlis
Kangar
Arau
Kuala Perlis
PERLIS
② Pulau Payar Marine Park
Alor Star
Kuala Kedah
KEDAH
Keroh
Baling
Gerik
Temenggor Lake
④ Belum and Temenggor Forest Reserves

Kota Bharu
Pangkal Kalong
Tanah Merah
S. Kelantan
Pulau Redang Marine Park
Kg. Penarik
⑮
⑭ Setiu
Kg. Merang
Kuala Terengganu

Georgetown
PULAU PINANG
Butterworth
Kulim
Bukit Mertajam
Kenering
KELANTAN
⑬ Ulu Kelantan
Gua Musang
Kenering Lake

Kenyir Lake
TERENGGANU
Kuala Dungun

Taiping
Kuala Kangsar
Ipoh
PERAK
S. Perak
Tanah Rata
⑤ Cameron Highlands Wildlife Sanctuary
Tapah

Taman Negara
Gn. Tahan ⑫ 2187m (7186ft) Airstrip
S. Tembeling
⑪ Taman Rimba Kenong
Kuala Lipis
Kuala Tembeling
Jerantut

Teluk Intam
Fraser's Hill ⑥
Tanjung Malim
SELANGOR
Gn. Benom 2107m (6913ft)
PAHANG
⑩ Krau Wildlife Reserve
Kuala Krau
Kuantan

PENINSULAR MALAYSIA

Kuala Selangor Nature Park ⑦
S. Selangor
Rawang
International Airport
Kuala Lumpur
Kelang
Karak
S. Pahang
Temerloh
Tasik Bera

NEGERI SEMBILAN
Seremban
Sepang
New International Airport
Port Dickson
MELAKA
Melaka
Muar
S. Muar
Segamat
Labis

S. Rompin
Kuala Rompin
⑨ Pulau Tioman Marine Park
Endau Rompin National Park ⑧
Gn. Besar ▲ 1036m (3400ft)
Mersing

Keluang
JOHOR
S. Johor
Batu Pahat
Senai
Johor Bahru
Changi

SINGAPORE

KEY

———	Main road
BRUNEI	International boundary
- - - - -	State boundary
Kuala Lumpur ◉	City or major town
Seremban ○	Village or small town
S. Teku	Water feature
Gn.Rabung 2187m ▲ (7186ft)	Peak in metres (feet)
✈	Airport

PENINSULAR MALAYSIA

0 — 50 — 100 km
0 — 25 — 50 miles

SARAWAK AND SABAH (BORNEO)

0 — 100 — 200 km
0 — 50 — 100 miles

N

The National Parks and Other Wild Places of Malaysia

PENINSULAR MALAYSIA

Peninsular Malaysia consists of eleven states, and the Federal Territory of Kuala Lumpur, in total occupying 131,612 square kilometres (50,815 square miles). It has a coastline of 2,016 kilometres (1,252 miles), including all the smaller offshore islands.

The most striking topographical feature is the Main Range, running roughly north to south, with several peaks exceeding 2,000 metres (6,500 feet). To the west of the Main Range, towards the Straits of Melaka, is a relatively narrow coastal plain, and to the east a much broader area of lowlands and ranges to both west and east.

Hilly ground occupies about half the land area and is still largely under natural forest cover. The forest shows a clear zonal succession, from mangroves on the coast through freshwater swamp and peat swamp forest, lowland dipterocarp forest, hill dipterocarp forest up to approximately 915 metres (3,000 feet), upper dipterocarp forest, lower montane forest and upper montane forest.

Of the Peninsula's parks the biggest and best known is Taman Negara, the first national park to be gazetted in Malaysia and renowned the world over for its rain forests and exceptionally rich wildlife. It has the distinction, too, of containing the Peninsula's highest mountain, Gunung Tahan, a popular climb. Hill-lovers can also enjoy tranquillity on the wooded slopes of the Cameron Highlands, where great tea estates form part of the magnificent scenery. At coastal level, in parks such as Kuala Selangor, there are mangrove swamps to explore and abundant birdlife to watch. The Peninsula's parks also include seas and islands – Pulau Tioman and the Pulau Redang group are just two important areas whose spectacular coral reefs and marine life are now protected.

THE LANGKAWI ISLANDS

A Tropical Refuge

The Langkawi group is a cluster of islands – 99 of them visible at high tide, and about 104 at low tide. Pulau Langkawi itself covers 320 square kilometres (123 square miles) and is the biggest island off the shores of Peninsular Malaysia. Other relatively big islands in the group include Pulau Dayang Bunting and Pulau Tuba, whilst the remainder are much smaller. The scenery is an interesting mixture of limestone and sandstone outcrops, clothed in greenery and surrounded by the blue sea. The Langkawi islands are rich in legends that form an integral part of Malay culture. Best known is the Legend of Mahsuri, a married woman wrongly accused of adultery and put to death. When the executioner plunged a dagger into her, white blood spurted from the wound as a sign of her innocence, and in her death throes Mahsuri put a curse on the island such that it would not prosper or enjoy peace for seven generations. Today, her curse no longer appears to be in effect and Langkawi is enjoying increasing prosperity from its development as a tourist destination.

Opposite: *Langkawi offers a unique combination of forest, limestone caves, lakes, beaches and sea.*

Above right: *The Malay Lacewing is a common butterfly of open areas.*

Previous pages
Page 20: *Tropical evergreen rain forest covers nearly half of Peninsular Malaysia.* Page 21: *The tiger: charismatic, endangered, and now the subject of intensive research.*

Pulau Langkawi

Pantai Cenang, formerly a rice-growing district backed inland by the very rustic settlements of Padang Matsirat, is the site of most visitor accommodation. It is possible to walk from here at low tide across the sandbar to the small island of Pulau Rebak, but you will be cut off if the tide comes in.

On Langkawi, Gunung Raya is the tallest natural feature, at 881 metres (2,890 feet). On this conical mountain is a telecommunications station and there is a small road to the top. As it is still forested, an adventurous trek is possible – for example, from the recreational site at Lubuk Sembilang to the peak. The plant and animal life is mainly a reduced selection of that found on the Peninsular Malaysian mainland, but with some unusual island endemics. Langkawi is particularly well known for having various butterflies different from those found in most of Peninsular Malaysia. Teak is one of the plants that prefer this seasonal climate, and you can see spectacular examples of flowering tree species that never blossom so well elsewhere in the country.

Other interesting plants, for example begonias, members of the African violet family and a rare fan palm, can be found on sandstone and sandstone-derived soils, especially in the northwest of Langkawi. Here are some of the oldest known rock formations in Malaysia, part of the Machinchang Range, about 2,500 million years old. Gunung Machinchang rises in a spectacular skyline of crags that glow pink in the sunset, and a guided trek can take you over parts of this range from north to south of the island.

Location: 24 km (15 miles) off the coast of Kedah, northwest Peninsular Malaysia.

Climate: Hot and humid all year, with a fairly predictable dry period about June–July. Usually hot by day and warm by night.

When to Go: Best between March and September, avoiding rougher seas and wetter weather at other times.

Access: Overland from Kuala Lumpur to Alor Star then bus or taxi to Kuala Perlis; by ferry to main town of Kuah. Alternatively, fly direct to Langkawi from Kuala Lumpur or Penang.

Permits: Not required.

Equipment: Diving or snorkelling equipment, beach gear, walking gear. Climbing or caving equipment if you are serious about tackling the limestone.

Facilities: As Langkawi is a large island, with villages, hotels and shops as well as wild places, virtually all facilities can be obtained or arranged on the spot. All ranges of accommodation from luxury to village homestay. Car hire available for getting around. Hotel owners can usually advise on making boat bookings.

Watching Wildlife: Diving and snorkelling may reveal sea life; dolphins sometimes visible from boats. Bats inhabit various caves (notably on west side of Pulau Dayang Bunting), and many important limestone-inhabiting plants occur. Pulau Singa Besar for semi-wild released animals.

Visitor Activities: Swimming, sunbathing, exploring caves. Walk to peak of Gunung Raya via forest route (a guide is advisable). Boat trips to various islands, popularly to Dayang Bunting and to Singa Besar but many other possibilities. For the adventurous, a guided trek over Gunung Machinchang is possible.

Map labels:
Datai Bay · Teluk Datai · Gn.Machinchang · Telaga Tujuh Falls · 708m (2322ft) · Gn.Sawak · 410m (1345ft) · Padang Matsirat · Pulau Langkawi · Pulau Rebak Besar · Pasir Hitam · Durian Peranginan Falls · Gn.Raya · 881m (2890ft) · Kuah · Pulau Langgun · Pulau Timun · Ferry to Kuala Perlis · Pantai Cenang · Pulau Tuba · Pulau Kentut Kecil · Pulau Dayang Bunting · Pulau Singa Besar · Kuala Lumpur · N

Between Pantai Cenang and Gunung Machinchang is Telaga Tujuh, the Seven Wells Waterfall. The climb from the lower falls becomes increasingly scenic the higher you go, but the rocks can be extremely slippery here and care is needed.

Spectacular Limestone

Langkawi is famous for its limestone, with many outcrops on the main island and others rising directly from the sea. Pulau Singa Kecil, for example, though hardly worth landing on, is nevertheless a fine sight, and others like Pulau Jong are even more photogenic. Off the eastern side of Pulau Tuba is a small island with a limestone arch, under which a small boat can pass at low tide. At high water, passengers must remember to duck.

Some limestone hills on the eastern side of Langkawi are set most unusually within the mangrove forests of the Kisap estuary. These hills are a very important conservation feature, with bats inside caves, rare and endemic snails and trapdoor spiders on the surface of the limestone, and many fine plants. The palm *Maxburretia rupicola* is confined to limestone habitats, and can be seen clinging to vertical rocks just a few metres above the sea.

Other Islands

Pulau Dayang Bunting, the second largest island, has Malaysia's best-known lake, Tasik Dayang Bunting. Said to be fresh water, it is in fact very slightly brackish. Another, smaller, freshwater lake is found on Pulau Langgun, reached only by a rather dangerous trek over sharp limestone rocks. An important conservation feature of Pulau Langgun is the presence of relatively large, intact fossils such as snail shells within the limestone.

Between Pulau Dayang Bunting and Pulau Tuba is the most extensive area of mangroves in the Langkawi group, but it is almost never visited except by a few local fishermen. The inland areas of the two islands are also little visited, and should prove rewarding. Large caves occur on the western side of Pulau Dayang Bunting. However, the forest here can be a dense tangle, with

climbers strung around trees that grow in clefts amongst jagged rock.

One island, Pulau Singa Besar, is managed as a sanctuary for animals, including some purposely released, such as mousedeer and peacocks. It has become a routine stop for many tour groups, but the truly wild Langkawi can be found elsewhere: in hill treks; in a circuit round the crumbling shales of the western coast; or in diving around some of the lesser-explored limestone and coral reefs. Up until now the small islands have all been poorly explored. Important geological features, such as the black sands of the northeastern coast and signs of crustal shifting among the offshore sandstone outcrops, await the informed observer.

Above: Many islands in the Langkawi group are of rugged limestone, with hidden sandy beaches.

Right: There is no shortage of holiday activities from the forest to the sea; fossicking on the shore is always fun.

PULAU PAYAR MARINE PARK

A Treasurehouse of Corals

Pulau Payar is the largest in a group of four islands (the others being Pulau Kaca, Selembu and Segantang), about 1.7 kilometres (1 mile) long and with a total area of 31 hectares (76 acres). It is narrow and the entire length of the northwestern coast is predominantly rocky, characterized by formidable steep cliffs and wave-cut gullies. Much of the island is covered with lush green vegetation, while its few small, sandy beaches are white and silkily fine-grained. The other three islands are not much more than rock outcrops, but their small size belies the wonderful treasures they house beneath their clear turquoise waters.

Pristine Coral Reefs

The Pulau Payar group constitutes one of the few pristine coral reef areas off the west coast of Peninsular

Opposite, top left: *Orange tube corals spread their arms wide to feed.*

Opposite, centre left: *The gills of the sea slug* Hypselodoris bullocki *stand up in a great orange tuft.*

Opposite, bottom left: *Sharp yellow spicules of calcium help defend these soft corals from predation.*

Opposite, right: *Around a branching colony of corals, the fragile tentacle of a brittlestar slowly coils.*

Above, right: *The park's jetty allows mooring without damage to the superb corals.*

Malaysia. A wide variety of habitat types is found within a relatively small area, and the coral is representative of the Indian Ocean, unlike the reefs off the east coast of the Peninsula. The islands' surrounding waters were gazetted as a Marine Park as early as 1985, giving the area the distinction of being the first park of its kind in Peninsular Malaysia.

The shallow waters of the park contain a luxuriant and diverse growth of as many as 35 hard coral genera, in all shapes and sizes. Particularly distinctive are the massive boulder corals off the southeastern coast of Pulau Payar. Spreading beds of stagshorn coral interspersed with table and encrusting corals, sponges and sea anemones support a multitude of marine life around the islands.

South of Pulau Payar lies a breathtakingly beautiful spot known as Coral Garden, where the colourful soft corals that predominate on the rocky underwater seascape offer an unforgettable view, that looks as though it had been planted for our enjoyment. Diverse coral can also be found around Pulau Kaca, particularly on its north and northeast sides. Some boats, impounded for illegal fishing, have been sunk off Pulau Kaca and these make an interesting wreck dive. Pulau Segantang, whose precipitous sides continue underwater to depths of over 10 metres (33 feet) before sloping gently to the sea floor, offers a topographically different underwater environment, and correspondingly different coral lifeforms for divers to explore through wall dives.

Location: 28 km (18 miles) off the coast of Kedah, and 34 km (21 miles) southeast of Kuah in Langkawi. The chain of islands is spread over a 16-km (10-mile) band of sea.

Climate: Usually hot by day throughout the year, but cool days are commoner in the wet period from November–March.

When to Go: Best between March and September, avoiding rougher seas in other months.

Access: By fast catamaran, once per day from Langkawi to the pontoon at Pulau Payar.

Permits: Not required in advance, all travel and access arrangements can be made on the spot.

Equipment: Light outdoor clothing, with a sun-hat and sunblock cream. Take snorkelling and diving gear according to your skills; rental of some such equipment is possible either in Langkawi or at Pulau Payar.

Facilities: Marine Park Centre with staff, information, video screenings, picnic tables, lavatories. Floating pontoon with snorkelling and diving facilities, underwater observatory, glass-bottomed boat rides, sunbathing deck and restaurant. There is no overnight accommodation.

Watching Wildlife: The great attractions are underwater; the Coral Garden for highly diverse corals, Pulau Kaca for wreck dives, Pulau Segantang for sloping reefs. There is little of interest on land except for some birdwatching.

Visitor Activities: Scuba diving, snorkelling and underwater photography are all rewarding.

Myriad Species of Fish

The park's greatest treasures are the fish. Myriad species abound, with large schools of colourful reef fish swirling amongst the intricate nooks and crannies of the reefs. The area is a breeding and nursery ground for many species. Barracuda, jacks, groupers, fusiliers, rabbitfish, snappers and damselfish are common, while the more elusive Whale Shark necessitates a bit of luck in finding it. The park is well known for its Blacktip Reef Sharks, and many juveniles congregate at the shallow bay in front of the Marine Park Centre. Beautiful and graceful in motion, the blacktips command due respect as they glide effortlessly through the water but they have not been known to pose a threat to divers.

Left: *The topography of the reef is more diverse than any terrestrial landscape.*

Below: *The main beach at Pulau Payar fronts an extensive shallow reef.*

Opposite, right: *The spiny Zebra Lionfish is a spectacular inhabitant of the reef.*

A Unique Diving Centre

As a tourist destination, Pulau Payar is unique among the other marine parks in Malaysia in that it houses Langkawi Coral, a 50-metre by 15-metre (165 x 50-foot) floating pontoon which is moored off the beach south of the Park Centre. The pontoon, the only one of its kind in the country, is serviced once daily by a fast catamaran from Pulau Langkawi, and offers visitors a luxury one-stop centre for reef-related activities.

Pulau Payar is uninhabited, the only building on the island being the tastefully rustic Marine Park Information Centre. Although small, the centre provides some visitor facilities and park staff are always on hand to help. It is possible to camp on one of the beaches on Pulau Payar, although permission has to be sought from the Department of Fisheries.

By far the most popular activity in the inviting waters of the park is snorkelling, although the more adventurous visitor might opt to venture deeper by scuba diving.

First-time divers need not fear, as introductory courses are offered. Underwater photography is another worthwhile pursuit that deepens the appreciation of the coral reef environment.

Research and Conservation

Pulau Payar Marine Park is important to many people for many reasons. Like the other marine parks in the country it is crucial for fisheries management and the conservation of biological diversity. The coral reefs of the area offer marine scientists and students an opportunity to conduct important research. Studies have been carried out there by various organizations including Universiti Sains Malaysia, WWF Malaysia and the Fisheries Research Institute. In addition, tourism, when sustainably managed, also generates a secure income for the area.

Above: *Most visitors use the Langkawi Coral pontoon as a base from which to explore the reef.*

Above: *The Freckled Hawkfish can be found among the branches of hard corals.*

PERLIS

Conservation in Malaysia's Smallest State

Nestling in the northernmost corner of Peninsular Malaysia is the country's smallest state, Perlis. Although only 795 square kilometres (307 square miles), it has much to offer the traveller. One attraction is a state park now being created, along the northern end of the Nakawan Range of hills, on the state's western border with Thailand.

This new park, the Nakawan State Park, is managed by the Perlis State Forestry Department. It is a spectacular place with enclosed valleys, jagged limestone peaks, rugged landscape and many caves. It is part of a continuous 300 square kilometres (115 square miles) of forest extending into Thailand, where it is under the protection of the adjacent Thaleban National Park.

Plants and Wildlife

Many plants growing directly on the limestone have adapted to the peculiarly dry conditions here. Two found nowhere else in Malaysia are the Gouty Balsam, with a great, bulbous water-storing stem, and the cactus-like

Opposite, top: The shallow Timah Tasoh Lake is proving important for waterbirds such as the Cotton Pygmy Goose.

Opposite, bottom left: The female Rhinoceros Hornbill has a white eye, the male a red.

Opposite, bottom right: Great Hornbills have a mainly northerly distribution in the Peninsula.

Above, right: White-handed Gibbons are confined to the taller forest.

Euphorbia. Perlis is itself the driest state in Malaysia, and the forest here is partly deciduous, known to botanists as white *meranti gerutu* forest after some of its typical tree species.

Wide open spaces covered with ricefields add colour to the scenery, the brilliant green of the young plants turning to gold before the harvest. Visitors may be able to help with planting and enjoy themselves splashing in the mud alongside the local farmers.

The park is the only place in Malaysia where the Stump-tailed Macaque can be found, a hefty monkey with a red face and red bottom. Four other species of primates, the wild goat known as Serow, leopards, wild pigs, and at least 30 other species of mammals are found throughout the park. There may be over 200 species of birds, including six kinds of hornbills, and at least 49 species of reptiles and amphibians. Most of the animals are hard to spot, but with a little effort you can find the White-handed Gibbon, Dusky Leaf-monkey and Long-tailed Macaque. Rare bats occur in some of the caves, and feed over the agricultural land during the night.

Trails and Caves

Although the park has yet to have its official status confirmed, some of its facilities, including its headquarters, have already been put in place by the state government. A trail system is also open which takes the visitor to the caves, to the local limestone peaks, and through beautiful forests. Some of the trails are steep and require the visitor to be reasonably fit.

Location: The northernmost state in Malaysia, about 6° 30' N, adjacent to the Thailand border.

Climate: Usually very hot by day, drier than most other parts of Malaysia.

When to Go: Any time of year.

Access: From Kuala Lumpur by train to Kangar, or by road along the North-South Highway (Route 1) for 380 km (240 miles) before following signs to Kangar. By air from Kuala Lumpur to Alor Star, and taxi from there to Kangar.

Permits: Not required, except for access to forested areas (apply to State Forestry Department in Kangar).

Equipment: Light outdoor clothing with light walking shoes. If you go caving or climbing, bring your own specialized equipment.

Facilities: As Perlis is an entire state, with varied towns, villages and rural areas, no general description is possible. A wide range of accommodation is available in the main town, Kangar, and some may be found at Kuala Perlis and Arau.

Watching Wildlife: Caves for bats; Timah Tasoh dam for ducks, grebe and other waterbirds; limestone hills for special rare plants. Ricefields can be good for open country birdwatching.

Visitor Activities: Caving, wildlife watching, but relatively few other activities are directly related to nature. Perlis is fascinating culturally (there are archaeological remains) and the Malaysian Tourism Promotion Board in Kangar can advise on cultural events. Historical tin-miners' trail can be followed at Wang Mu.

Right: *Formidable limestone outcrops are juxtaposed with rice-growing areas of the coastal plain.*

Above: *Perlis is the southernmost limit of the Stumptailed Macaque's range.*

Below: *Limestone provides harsh growing conditions for plants, and many species are unique to this habitat.*

The park is about 30 kilometres (19 miles) from the state capital, Kangar, by good metalled road. Padang Besar, the major entry point from Thailand, is only 15 kilometres (9 miles) away. From here buses and taxis are available to take you to Kaki Bukit, the nearest town to the park. Another entry point from Thailand is through Thaleban National Park, which will take the traveller straight to Wang Kelian. From here transport to the park headquarters is limited to taxis.

Upon arriving at Kaki Bukit, walk to Gua Kelam and go through the 380-metre (415-yard) cave. This is lighted and the pathway is a suspended boardwalk above an underground stream. The park headquarters are situated another 10 minutes' walk beyond the cave, and are signposted. They are located in a hidden, enclosed valley called Wang Tangga (Valley of the Steps).

Timah Tasoh Lake

There are many other places in Perlis that are worth a visit. About 130 species of birds can be found at the scenic Timah Tasoh Lake north of Kangar, and the list is growing. The northern end of the lake is where most birds can be found. The best time for birdwatching is during the migratory periods, about November and March, when wild ducks, grebe, egrets, herons, kingfishers and raptors are easier to spot.

BELUM AND TEMENGGOR FOREST RESERVES

Lakeside Camps and Jungle Trekking

Together, the Belum and Temenggor Forest Reserves cover an enormous 2,000 square kilometres (772 square miles). They lie respectively north and south of the highway that cuts through the forest of northern Peninsular Malaysia from Perak into Kelantan, and they have been further separated since 1977 by the waters of Temenggor Lake, created by the construction of a dam for hydro-electricity. A combination of open water, excellent forest and rich wildlife provides the area's attractiveness.

Access to the forest reserves is via the island of Banding, where there is a resthouse for visitors. Several small tourism businesses have been set up here, with floating chalets for fishing holidays. Recently, Banding has been identified for major tourism developments, but it is still possible to use the island merely as a take-off point for journeys across the lake.

Trekking from the Lake

The lake is nearly 100 metres (330 feet) deep near the dam, but only the top few metres of water are really suitable for fish. The productive parts are the little inlets formed where a stream plunges down a slope from the forest into the lake. The mixing of the water here encourages the growth of algae and other water-plants, so that fish and frogs, water snails and water boatmen all occur in abundance. Look out for otters, kingfishers and other wildlife in these secluded inlets.

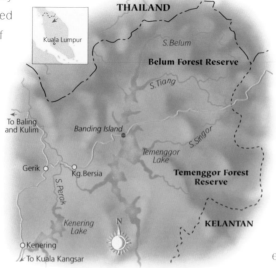

From Banding, camping trips, fishing and forest treks can be arranged, which involve a boat trip across the lake. Several campsites have been established near to points where streams debouch into the lake. These sites offer all the advantages of a clean water supply, access to the lake for canoeing and cool, quiet shady forest.

Starting to walk uphill from such a camp, the visitor will find very varied features. By the stream it is damp and humid, rocky, sometimes rather slippery, with a dense understorey of ferns, wild peppers, arrowroots, gingers and wild yams. The climb can be tricky, especially when clambering up or round one of the many cascades.

On the ridgetops, the scene is very different. Here there are more big trees, a scanty and open understorey with stemless palms, wider views and altogether drier conditions. Walking the ridges can involve long muscle-aching hauls, but it can be immensely exciting if you encounter recent traces of large mammals such as elephants or tigers.

The Fruit Tree Harvest

Wild fruit trees are amongst the specialities of the Belum area. There are durians, mangoes, jackfruits, rambutans, lemons and many others. Their abundance here helps to

Above, right: *Scattered within the forest are durian trees of truly wild and semi-domesticated forms, the fruits come under traditional ownership.*

Location: Northernmost part of the state of Perak, abutting border with Thailand, about 300 km (190 miles) from Kuala Lumpur.

Climate: Hot by day, somewhat cool by night; similar throughout the year but with scattered rain and wet periods especially from October–February.

When to Go: Any time of year.

Access: By car, bus or outstation taxi. From Kuala Lumpur on the North-South Highway to Kuala Kangsar, then north to Gerik and east to Banding Island. From Penang, Gerik can be reached by road via Kulim and Baling.

Permits: Banding, an island in Temenggor Lake, is a public access point. Arrange with police station in Gerik for permission to venture into forest south of the highway at Banding; forest to the north is generally out of bounds.

Equipment: Light clothing, a hat, walking shoes, poncho, sunblock cream and swimming gear. Camping or fishing equipment as required.

Facilities: There is resthouse accommodation at Banding, with food stalls. Several operators have made floating fishing lodges at Temenggor Lake, some have chalets on islands, all simple affairs. Boats can be arranged with such operators from Banding.

Watching Wildlife: Arrange forest camping to look for birds and other wildlife; much has been seen in the area including elephants, Gaur, bears, tiger, deer, a full range of monkeys and gibbons, and (occasionally spectacular) congregations of hornbills. On the lake, look out for eagles and other birds in dead trees.

Visitor Activities: Walking, camping, fishing, birdwatching and boating.

Above: *The biggest gatherings of Wreathed Hornbills in the world have been seen over Temenggor Lake.*

Right: *The most rural settlements are built entirely of materials from the forest.*

Opposite: *Tigers, the largest and most formidable of predators in the forest, have been seen by a few lucky visitors.*

Below, right: *Sungai Sara, where floating chalets have been built, is one of several visitor destinations.*

explain an equal abundance of animals, for monkeys such as Long-tailed and Pig-tailed Macaques seem to be especially common. Elephants use the ridges as travel routes, stopping to browse on the fallen fruit, rattans and gingers. Wild pigs grub amongst the leaf litter in company with ground-living rats and porcupines, taking advantage of the seeds dropped from the canopy by monkeys, squirrels and gibbons.

August seems to be the best month at Belum for fruiting trees, and it is probably no coincidence that this is also the time when big concentrations of hornbills start to appear. From time to time between August and the end of the year, small flocks of Wreathed Hornbills gradually come together and head for a common roosting area. Wave after wave may pass overhead, then settle briefly before moving on again. During a Malaysian Nature Society expedition to Temenggor in 1993, the best count was more than 2,500 hornbills on a single evening. Together with the impressive number of big mammals, the hornbill phenomenon makes the region one of tremendous importance for conservation.

Secret Life of the Forest

On the steep hills, bamboo is common wherever there has been an old landslide. Some of the bamboo stems can reach 15 centimetres (6 inches) in diameter, and these hollow canes are inhabited by a world of different creatures. Small beetles and some ants can bore holes into the bamboo and live inside. Larger holes permit the

Above: *The abundance of fruits encourages wildlife such as Pig-tailed Macaques.*

entry of Flat-headed Bats, which have flattened skulls that enable them to squeeze through very narrow gaps. If rainwater happens to collect inside the bamboo, it may form a home for mosquito larvae, but one species of ant is able to suck up the water bit by bit and spit it outside.

The forest around Belum and Temenggor is full of such oddities, and they are much commoner than the spectacular tigers or elephants which everyone hopes to see. You will find that getting down on your hands and knees to look for little creatures is worth the effort.

Arranging a Trip

The forests of Belum and Temenggor are contained within permanent reserves managed by the State Forestry Department. For the outsider, the simplest way of arranging a trip is to contact one of the established tour operators in the area, and allow them to obtain or advise on relevant permits. Some companies may have standing arrangements with the management agencies, or be willing to handle the permissions needed. Access to the Temenggor Lake is simple, and as tourism expands so travel and camping arrangements are becoming easier.

Visitors are best advised to head south from Banding Island. Guides are more familiar with this area, and navigation across and around the lake is easier. Most of the sightings of big mammals have been in this area, and from here you will have closer access to known salt licks and the limestone outcrops to the south.

CAMERON HIGHLANDS WILDLIFE SANCTUARY

Hill Forests and Tea Plantations

C ameron Highlands, the smallest administrative district in the state of Pahang, rises to between 600 and 2,032 metres (1,968–6,667 feet), and includes the most nearly level highland plateau area in Peninsular Malaysia. The area was discovered by a surveying party led by William Cameron in 1885.

In the years after this discovery, Cameron Highlands was developed as a cool hill station and tea plantations, rest houses for holidays, and various other developments were established. The three main towns are Tanah Rata, Brinchang and Ringlet. Although lately continuing development has been quite rapid, it is largely concentrated on the gentler western flanks of the Main Range, leaving much of the steeper eastern slopes as yet untouched. Because of its importance, Cameron Highlands was gazetted as a Wildlife Sanctuary in 1962, covering 649 square kilometres (251 square miles). It is an outstanding example of the montane environment, with many known endemic species of plants.

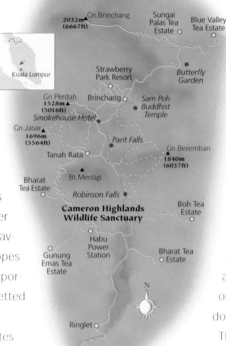

Montane Forests

From upper hill dipterocarp forest at the lesser altitudes, there is a transition to lower montane forest rich in tropical oaks and laurels, then to upper montane forest with stunted, mossy vegetation on the mountain summits. Rhododendrons, pitcher plants and lipstick plants can be found in the forest, growing on the ground or on other plants, and wild orchids are abundant. Endemic species of the tiny helmet orchids grow amongst the moss, and rare and threatened slipper orchids occur on the slopes lower down. All are protected.

The keen-eyed visitor will be able to find many species of interesting birds, including all but one of the 74 montane specialists found in Peninsular Malaysia. Some of these, like the Rufous-bellied Niltava and Chestnut-winged Minla, are confined to the upper montane environment, and so do not occur at the slightly lower altitude hill stations such as Fraser's Hill.

Black panthers find the undisturbed forest ideal, and the closely related Clouded Leopard is also found here. Both these elusive animals are rare sightings, but their tracks can sometimes be seen. Wild cats, wild boar, the Serow or mountain goat, civets and other mammals are

Opposite, top left: The shrubby Agapetes scortechinii occurs near the highest peak of Cameron Highlands, Gunung Brinchang.

Opposite, centre left: Rarely seen, the Clouded Leopard is one of the top predators.

Opposite, bottom left: Many gingers such as Amomum flower on the forest floor.

Opposite, right: Ridges are the favoured site for small aboriginal villages.

Above, right: The Temiar people inhabit adjoining parts of Pahang, Kelantan and Terengganu.

Location: At 1,200–1,800 m (4,000–6,000 ft) on the spine of the Main Range, 160 km (100 miles) north of Kuala Lumpur.

Climate: Warm by day, often cold at night, generally a temperate climate with some mist and drizzle at all seasons. Wetter weather tends to occur in April–May and November–February.

When to Go: Any time of year, but March–September is best.

Access: By car, outstation taxi, bus to Tapah (or train to Tapah Road station). Then by road from Tapah to any of the main settlements at Cameron Highlands.

Permits: Not required.

Equipment: Light clothing, walking shoes, and some warmer clothing for evenings. A poncho or hat as protection from rain.

Facilities: A range of accommodation is available, mostly in the towns of Tanah Rata and Brinchang. Restaurants, shops, etc. Various signposted walking trails, from a few minutes to several hours, easy to strenuous. Maps are available at local shops.

Watching Wildlife: Forest birds and plants along the walking trails; especially look out for whistling thrushes and forktails along rocky streams; epiphytic ferns and orchids in the tall moist forest; elfin mossy forest on mountain peaks where many butterflies occur.

Visitor Activities: Forest and mountain walking, birdwatching, plant spotting, photography. Camping is not a usual activity here, though possible in some places for small groups. During travels, observe highland agriculture, flower growing. Tea estates can be visited; Boh tea factory open to the public on certain days, with guided tours.

Above: *Leopards occur up to high altitudes; of the two forms, black are more common here than spotted.*

Right and opposite: *Cameron Highlands form the country's premier site for tea production. The picking of tea shoots begins early in the cool mornings over the hills.*

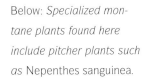

Below: *Specialized montane plants found here include pitcher plants such as* Nepenthes sanguinea.

present. Other wildlife in the montane forest is too diverse to catalogue, but includes a great variety of beetles, butterflies and moths. Among the snakes is the poisonous but attractive Wagler's Pit-viper, while the Silver Bronzeback and Copperhead Racer can sometimes be seen slithering away.

Trail Walking

There are several numbered trails that can be visited by even the most inexperienced trekker. They are concentrated mainly around the towns of Tanah Rata and Brinchang. One of the shortest walks is the paved footpath to Parit Falls, just outside Tanah Rata. Though the area is poorly maintained, it gives opportunities to see Slaty-backed Forktails, black-and-white thrushlike birds that favour rocks in the river, and Malayan Whistling Thrushes which are one of the few birds endemic to Peninsular Malaysia.

A longer trail leads from the outskirts of Tanah Rata to Robinson Falls. Look out for various wild flowers along the way, including the rare Malayan Violet. Some good sightings of birds can be made here. Green Magpie and Red-headed Trogon are occasionally seen in the adjacent trees. It is possible to continue on from the falls for a couple of hours to emerge near the Boh Tea plantation, about 12 kilometres (7 miles) from Tanah Rata. Cameron Highlands is locally famous for its tea, and this well-known estate can be visited. Amongst the tea bushes,

birds such as Silver-eared Mesias can be seen with smaller wildlife such as Anglehead lizards, while Large Cuckoo-shrikes may perch in the taller trees.

Possibly the best of all the agricultural scenery is found at Sungai Palas, above the town of Brinchang. A steep walk from Brinchang to the telecommunications station at the top of Gunung Brinchang (2,032 metres/6,667 feet) will take you through tea plantations and lower montane forest to the stunted upper montane forest at the summit. An observation tower there gives splendid views of the surrounding peaks and vegetation, and of birds flying over the low forest canopy, but it is often misty.

Summit Routes

Gunung Irau is a mountain peak on the border between Pahang and Perak. The most accessible route to the summit begins at an open, sandy, roadside spot a short distance below the peak of Gunung Brinchang. This trail runs along the ridge of the saddle between the two mountains. The ascent and return can take most of a day, and leads through some of the most beautiful mossy forest available.

The mountain known as Gunung Swettenham is on the periphery of Cameron Highlands, and the ascent would usually require an overnight stay. This climb can be challenging for beginners but is quite safe, though it is wise to employ a guide familiar with the trails.

FRASER'S HILL

A Tranquil Hill Resort

Fraser's Hill, at about 1,200 metres (3,900 feet) altitude, is approximately halfway along the Main Range, on the border between the states of Selangor and Pahang. This is one of the three most popular hill resorts in the country, and is the oldest. It is also the least developed, and a great part of its charm is that most of its environment and natural landscapes are intact. The highest point within the immediate vicinity of the Fraser's Hill settlement is at the High Pines Bungalow, about 1,280 metres (4,200 feet). There are some seven nearby peaks which exceed this altitude, notably Pine Tree Hill at 1,448 metres (4,750 feet).

Lying at this relatively moderate elevation, and surrounded by hill and lower montane forest, Fraser's Hill preserves an ambience of peace and tranquillity. It is particularly popular with birdwatchers and other wildlife enthusiasts as well as appealing to city dwellers who wish to escape for the weekend.

Opposite, top left: Among migrant birds at Fraser's Hill is the Blue-winged Pitta.

Opposite, bottom left: Little Cuckoo-doves nest in the mountains, but often feed lower down the hillslopes during the day.

Opposite, right: Great birdwatching is possible along the marked forest trails.

Above right: Large Niltavas, brilliantly coloured flycatchers common in montane forests, can be seen alone or in groups of other bird species.

Bird Diversity

Fraser's Hill is internationally recognized amongst the birding community. Some 263 species of birds have been recorded, which is one of the highest counts of birds living in montane forest in the country. Out of the strictly montane species (many others are essentially lowland birds that can also survive in the mountains), most have affinities with the Himalayan region. Examples of these are the Cutia, White-browed Shrike-babbler and Large Niltava.

A geographical peculiarity of Fraser's Hill is that it is situated at the point where there is a kink in the overall north-south orientation of the Main Range. Many birds on migration cross the range of mountains at this bend, and some of them stop over in the montane forest. Species such as the Eyebrowed Thrush feed in the forest, taking berries and figs, whilst others such as the Blue-winged Pitta fly over at night on their way to or from their non-breeding quarters in the lowlands.

Botanical Riches

Fraser's Hill is renowned as a floristically rich and important site, by virtue of its many endemic plants as well as the overall total of species. A recently published survey found just over 900 species of flowering plants, nearly one-third of which are limited to the Peninsula, and at least 31 occur only at Fraser's Hill. Four prime conservation sites have been identified for plants, each of them accessible to the public along the road and trail system. Of special conservation interest is the ancient trig oak, which is known from only three sites in the world, at Fraser's Hill, Gunung Kinabalu, and Sulawesi.

Location: 105 km (65 miles) north of Kuala Lumpur, at 1,200 m (3,900 ft) on the spine of the Main Range mountains.

Climate: Usually pleasantly warm days, cool evenings and nights. Often misty with drizzle, especially October–March.

When to Go: Any time of year, but the weather is on average more pleasant from about March onwards.

Access: Travel by car, bus or taxi on the North-South Highway to Rawang, then follow the old road to Kuala Kubu Baru, then northeast to The Gap at 825 m (2,700 ft). The last 8 km (5 miles) from here to Fraser's Hill are on a gated road with one-way traffic uphill (odd hours) and downhill (even hours) by daylight. A new road is currently under construction.

Permits: Not required.

Equipment: Sturdy shoes and leech socks for forest walks, a poncho or light raincoat, and a pullover or jacket for chilly nights. Otherwise, cameras and binoculars according to taste.

Facilities: Good range of accommodation in hotels, or in classical bungalows (book via Fraser's Hill Development Corporation). Some visitors prefer to stay at The Gap Resthouse (book via District Office, Kuala Kubu Baru). Various long and short jungle trails are signposted; a nature education centre has been established.

Watching Wildlife: Birdwatching is good everywhere; wild boar are common in forest, and tigers have been seen. Trails are clearly signposted.

Visitor Activities: Walking, birdwatching, photography, observation of rare plants. International bird race in June.

Right: *The trails at Fraser's Hill look out over deep, forested valleys.*

Below: *The buzzing call of the Fire-tufted Barbet is frequently heard at Fraser's Hill.*

Getting Around

Since 1919, access to Fraser's Hill has been by a single narrow road. A gate system was imposed, whereby up traffic and down traffic were forced to alternate on an hourly schedule. Although some visitors find this part of the charm, a second road is near completion. Fraser's Hill is small enough for no internal public transport to be needed and it is easy to go everywhere on foot.

For nature lovers of all kinds, walking the seven established jungle trails is highly recommended. The popular Bishop's Trail is about 1.6 kilometres (1 mile) long, and takes about one and a half hours to walk at a moderate pace. Interesting encounters can be expected, from little crawling insects such as termites and beetles, to tiny herbaceous plants with colourful flowers, mosses and fungi, gingers, palms and rattans, lianas and epiphytes. One may observe or hear a variety of birds such as Long-tailed Broadbills or Orange-breasted Trogons, and other animals include squirrels, Banded Leaf-monkeys and Siamang.

Development and Conservation

The national and international biological importance of Fraser's Hill is reflected in its status. The portion of the

hills that falls within Selangor was made a Wildlife Sanctuary in 1922. The much larger portion in Pahang, now administered by the Town Board, was protected as a reserve under state legislation in 1957. The entire area is also protected within forest reserves. The Fraser's Hill Development Corporation, soon to be modified with an extended role in other parts of Pahang, is responsible for overseeing physical development, administration and tourism promotion. The corporation also maintains some of the accommodation facilities, which range from hotels and apartments to bungalows dating from the colonial period. Until recently, infrastructure develop-ment and traffic volumes have been light. The roads are narrow and winding as they were built mainly along con-tour lines. The high annual rainfall and the sandy quartz soils, which have little natural cohesion, are major con-straints to development.

A new nature education centre has been established by the Fraser's Hill Development Corporation in collabo-ration with WWF Malaysia, and much research is also undertaken, with a university ecological station and plans for an astronomical observatory. Permanent botanical plots have been set up to study the composi-tion, density and diversity of the montane flora.

Above: *At Fraser's Hill there is a transition from lowland birds such as the Gold-whiskered Barbet (bottom) to the montane Streaked Spiderhunter (centre) and Silver-eared Mesia (top).*

KUALA SELANGOR NATURE PARK

Coastal Birdlife and Mangrove Boardwalks

Kuala Selangor, a former royal town and the residence of the Sultans of Selangor, is the point at which the Sungai Selangor reaches the sea. The remains of the Sultans' fort can still be seen on the hill known as Bukit Melawati. This lookout now commands a splendid view over the Kuala Selangor Nature Park, on which work started in 1987.

Here about 324 hectares (800 acres) of land, between the coast and the town, has long been isolated from the sea by a bund (embankment) and canal, gradually changing from a mangrove-dominated community to one rich in fig-trees and other secondary growth. Offshore, the mudflats in the estuary are one of the most important spots in the country for cockle production, an industry partly dependent on the maintenance of healthy mangrove forests along the adjacent shore. The establishment of the park, it was hoped, would not only provide local townsfolk with a place for leisure and recreation, but also help to protect the coastline.

Opposite, top left: An observation tower at Kuala Selangor Nature Park makes a good wildlife lookout point.

Opposite, bottom left: Boardwalks passing through the mangroves provide opportunities for nature watching.

Opposite, right: The biggest kingfisher along the coast is the Stork-billed Kingfisher.

Above, right: Buffy Fish-owls nest in the larger trees and seek food along the shallow water margin.

The Mangrove Community

Mangroves are superb for nature watching. Fiddler crabs, the males each with one great colourful claw that they wave as a signal and warning to their rivals; pistol prawns, uncurling so quickly that they create a vacuum which is filled by water with a loud crack; mudskipper fish, flipping along the surface of the water to reach the next tree root, or defying each other with dramatic wriggles and unfurling of their sail-like, turquoise-spotted dorsal fins; these are common. Boardwalks leading from the coastal bund to the seaward edge of the mangroves enable all of these creatures to be seen without the discomfort of wading through thigh-deep mud. At the seaward end, you can stand and look out across the mudflats where, at low tide, there are likely to be Grey Herons, Great and Little and Intermediate Egrets, Redshanks and Mongolian Plovers and perhaps, in the distance, one of the few remaining Lesser Adjutant Storks.

Raptors and Waders

Along the coast, Brahminy Kites are one of the commonest big birds, and they depend on flotsam for much of their food. In the park it is rare not to see one overhead, and sometimes there are 40 or even more kites circling in the thermals. The White-bellied Sea-eagles that regularly nest on the radio tower on nearby Bukit Melawati (a Wildlife Reserve since 1922) can also be seen taking dead fish, but prefer live ones grappled from the waters of the estuary.

Location: 72 km (45 miles) northwest of Kuala Lumpur, on the west coast at the estuary of the Sungai Selangor.

Climate: Typical coastal lowlands weather, can be very hot by day and warm by night. Can rain at any time of year, but wet weather more likely in April–May and October–January.

When to Go: Good months for shorebirds are March and October, but there is always some wildlife to be seen.

Access: Travel by car, or by bus (Puduraya terminal) from Kuala Lumpur to Kuala Selangor town. Walk to the park from Bukit Melawati hill, or follow road signs past clinic to the park.

Permits: Not required. There is a small entrance fee.

Equipment: Light outdoor clothing, with a wide-brimmed hat, and light walking shoes. Sunblock cream is a good idea. Binoculars if you are birdwatching.

Facilities: Accommodation can be booked in advance via the Malaysian Nature Society, varying from simple chalets to extremely basic A-frame huts. Park office, shop, education facilities, self-catering facilities (check before you go). A range of trails, boardwalks in mangroves, bird hides, observation towers.

Watching Wildlife: Within the park more than 170 species of birds have been recorded. Keep a lookout for otters. Silvered Leaf-monkeys and Long-tailed Macaques are almost-guaranteed.

Visitor Activities: Birdwatching and monkey watching. At Kampung Kuantan (8 kilometres/5 miles away), watching spectacular fireflies at night. Seafood, pottery makers and historical sites add variety.

Above: *Milky Storks are the subject of a special conservation programme at Kuala Selangor.*

Above, right: *The shallow lake provides feeding opportunities for herons, egrets and other wildlife.*

Right: *The muddy coast and estuary offer plenty of food for scavenging Brahminy Kites.*

Opposite: *The vegetarian Silvered Leaf-monkeys, with their spectacular orange infants, are characteristic of coastal forest.*

Kuala Selangor is one in a chain of important stop-over points for migrating waders, that move along the west coast of the Peninsula twice a year. It is estimated that between 40,000 and 100,000 waders, of about 30 species, make the journey. Out of these, Redshanks are by far the commonest, with Curlew Sandpipers, Greater Sand-plovers and Mongolian Plovers also quite abundant, and birds such as the Asian Dowitcher, Nordmann's Greenshank and Spoon-billed Sandpiper extremely rare. Some will remain here all through the northern winter, others will continue south to Indonesia, or even further. Rarities and unusual sightings are not confined to the waders: Javan Pond-heron, Lineated Barbet and White-breasted Wood-swallows have been seen from time to time since the park opened.

Animal Watching

The mammals are important, too, in Kuala Selangor Nature Park. Silvered Leaf-monkeys live in troops of about 20, usually one or two males and plenty of females carrying their bright orange babies. Long-tailed Macaques, equally common, tend to live in bigger groups, with several adult males, and are inclined to be aggressive.

The park has a shallow lake, and now several bird hides and observation towers, and there is an extensive trail system, which gives access to all the habitat types but still leaves most of the park unvisited. At the park headquarters, managed by the Malaysian Nature Society on behalf of the Selangor state government, unprepared birdwatchers can hire binoculars.

Fireflies at Kampung Kuantan

Most visitors to Kuala Selangor combine their trip with a visit to Kampung Kuantan, 8 kilometres (5 miles) away. The fireflies in the riverside trees here are astonishing, clustering in hundreds within each suitable tree. They begin flashing around dusk, and only as it becomes darker, and the fireflies become better co-ordinated, does it suddenly become obvious that the males flash in synchrony. On moonless nights this is a really impressive spectacle, with tree after tree lighting up the river-bank. The firefly tours are operated by a local company whose staff work by group agreement on a democratic rota, a good example of community-based ecotourism. Research on the habitat requirements of the fireflies is still continuing.

ENDAU ROMPIN NATIONAL PARK

Between the Rivers and the Hills

Amongst the most isolated of Malaysia's mountain groups is that contained in one of its newest parks, Endau Rompin, established in 1989. The park covers 800 square kilometres (300 square miles), of which 489 square kilometres (189 square miles) are in Johor and the rest (known as Rompin Endau) is in Pahang. One reason why the Endau Rompin area is important is the presence of the Sumatran Rhinoceros. A few are still left here, but a sighting is very unlikely for any visitor. However, other big mammals, including elephants, tigers, leopards and Sambar Deer, occur and more than 200 species of birds have been recorded.

Notable features of Endau Rompin are the great variety of forest types supported by the granite-derived valleys, the sandstone hilltop plateaux, the cliffs and swampy patches. Also important are the plants, some unique to the park. About a dozen plants have been described from here within the last 15 years, by far the biggest and most spectacular of which is the fan-palm, *Livistona endauensis*. Others include several small herbs of the African violet family, and a beautiful little understorey tree with coppery coloured foliage.

The Johor Sector

Most visitors to the park arrive by four-wheel drive over dirt roads that were once logging tracks, giving access to the village of Kampung Peta. The people here are known as Orang Hulu, and their language is significantly different from the Malay spoken by their neighbours. From the village and park headquarters the best way into the park is by boat. Along the way it is often possible to see Long-tailed Macaques or a monitor lizard near the riverbank. Look for the cliffs, just visible as a line through the forest as though drawn with a ruler, along the flank of Gunung Janing.

At Kuala Jasin, the Sungai Endau and Sungai Jasin meet in a rocky and rather dangerous confluence, but just upstream there are some delightful bathing spots. From here, various trails can take the visitor, depending on stamina, to the riverine forest of Kuala Marong, the rapids of Jeram Upeh Guling, the waterfall of Buaya Sangkut, the hilltop of Gunung Janing, or – for the very determined – the distant plateau known as Padang Temambung.

At Kuala Marong, an hour's walk from the park headquarters, a scrap of alluvial forest supports some characteristic species, such as the Grey-breasted Babbler. One of the most striking features at Kuala Marong is the extraordinary clarity of the river there. It is shallow enough to paddle over comfortably. Nearby is the little mid-river island of Pulau Jasin, one of the botanical curiosities of

Opposite, top: The waters of the Sungai Endau can be of exceptional clarity.

Opposite, bottom left: Tigers, in small numbers, range throughout the park, in the forest and along trails.

Opposite, bottom centre: The lizard Calotes emma is gradually extending its range southwards.

Opposite, bottom right: River trips form an exciting part of the Endau Rompin experience.

Above, right: Endau Rompin is popular with the adventure-minded; many treks are physically demanding.

Location: In the southeast of Peninsular Malaysia, on the border of the states of Johor and Pahang, surrounded by the square of towns Segamat, Keluang, Mersing and Rompin.

Climate: Hot by day, usually warm by night, scattered days of rain throughout the year; generally more rain November–March.

When to Go: Any time of year, but occasional flooding of rivers can occur, perhaps more likely in February–March.

Access: Most easily by road from Kuala Lumpur or Singapore to Keluang, then east to beyond Kahang Baharu, and north to Kampung Nitar. Another road, from Kahang to Kampung Peta, is only suitable for 4-wheel drive vehicles. From Kampung Nitar or Kampung Peta, about 1 hour by boat to accommodation.

Permits: Must be arranged with National Parks Corporation (Johor) in Johor Bahru. If you are travelling with a tour operator, they may do this on your behalf.

Equipment: Light clothing, walking shoes, swimming gear, poncho. Some basic camping equipment is a good idea. Bring food supplies.

Facilities: Under development, Endau Rompin is not for the luxury-demanding tourist, but is rewarding for those seeking simple camp life, river-based activities and longer treks. Various trails lead to main places of interest. Guides can be obtained from Kampung Peta.

Watching Wildlife: Birdwatching anywhere; along trails, look out for signs of elephants, tigers and other big mammals.

Visitor Activities: Camping, swimming, birdwatching, walking along forest trails, fording rivers, and photography. Swim with discretion, bearing in mind fast currents.

the park. Periodically ripped over by floodwaters, the island still supports tough little trees and other plants, including various montane species which have managed to find a foothold just a few hundred metres above sea level. Abundant pitcher plants and orchids add to the montane atmosphere. On the trees are many epiphytes, some such as the Monkey's Head providing an internal network of passages which ants use for their nests.

Just upstream from the island are the rapids known as Jeram Upeh Guling. In the granite boulders that form the bed of the river here are almost perfectly round holes, up to a metre across, like natural bath-tubs made out of the rock. Two to three hours trek further upstream, at Buaya

Sangkut, the river makes a fierce plunge. From limpid green pools in the terraced rock above the falls, it suddenly drops 15 metres (50 feet) in a rage of white water. In the early morning, a cloud hovers just above the waterfall where the spray gathers. Visitors to this lovely spot should take care when exploring close to the river.

At Buaya Sangkut, and on Gunung Janing, the unique fan-palm, *Livistona endauensis*, predominates in the surrounding forest. It is a most impressive sight, but there is little in a fan-palm forest that animals can eat. A few gibbons and monkeys may pass through but will not stay, and a group of pigs, here often the unusual Bearded Pig, may come to forage through the leaf litter.

Conservation and New Discoveries

Thanks to work by the Department of Wildlife and National Parks since the 1970s, and expeditions by the Malaysian Nature Society in 1985 and 1989, more is known about Endau Rompin than any other park in Peninsular Malaysia. Besides the discovery of new species, many aspects of forest ecology on shallow sandstone soils and of riverine biology have been studied.

The Johor sector is now managed by the National Parks Corporation (Johor). This body is specifically charged with the creation, management and maintenance of a network of areas for conservation, research, education and recreation.

The Pahang sector of the park, Rompin Endau, is usually reached via dirt roads from the coastal town of Pontian, leading north of the flat-topped mountain Gunung Keriong, to the Sungai Kinchin. There is more alluvial forest here than in the Johor sector, and it contains various trees that are confined to the southern part of Peninsular Malaysia, including the white-flowered *Dillenia albiflos*. A rare bird here is the Giant Pitta.

Above: *The unique fan-palm* Livistona endauensis *grows in shallow soils on the hilltops.*

Top right: *Black and white colouring is found in a number of mainly nocturnal mammals such as the Malayan Tapir.*

Centre right: *Sambar stags give an explosive steam-engine whistle if alarmed by visitors.*

Bottom right: *Endau Rompin is famous for its Sumatran Rhinoceros, a few of which are still left here.*

Overleaf: *Rapids and calm water alternate through the park according to changing geology beneath the surface; the crossing near Kuala Jasin needs care.*

PULAU TIOMAN MARINE PARK

A Scattering of Coral Islands

Pulau Tioman is the third largest island off the coast of Peninsular Malaysia, and is part of a scattering of 64 islands in this southeastern area. The Pulau Tioman Marine Park encompasses the waters around Pulau Tioman itself, around the small offshore islands of Pulau Labas, Pulau Sepoi, Pulau Gut, Pulau Tokong Bahara, Pulau Chebeh and Pulau Tulai, as well as around Pulau Sembilang and Pulau Seri Buat which are further afield.

A Cloak of Forest

Most of Pulau Tioman, a Wildlife Reserve since 1972, is still covered in primary forest on slopes with steep gradients. These forests are a haven for many species of birds, bats, mousedeer, lizards, squirrels and myriad insects. At altitudes below about 610 metres (2,000 feet), lofty hardwood trees such as *Shorea* and *Dipterocarpus* are typical. The closed canopy provides dense shade from the heat of the day and the open forest floor has a sporadic understorey vegetation characterized by many exotic-looking shrubs and palms. In contrast, the montane forest in the zone above is made up of somewhat more stunted trees such as myrtles, laurels and heaths, all covered with a lush growth of ferns and lichens. Along the coastline, beach strand vegetation is characterized by carpeting

Opposite: Fine sandy beaches can be found on both east and west coasts of Pulau Tioman.

Above, right: Featherstars, related to starfishes, spend most of their lives clinging to other objects in the current.

creepers, low shrubs, coconut palms and casuarinas. Pulau Tioman also houses fragments of mangroves, mainly along the west coast of the island, especially in the vicinity of the village of Kampung Paya.

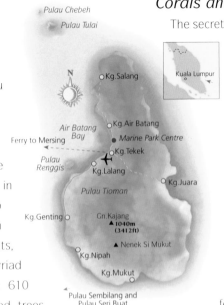

Corals and Marine Life

The secrets of the park are contained within its diverse coral reefs, whose beauty accentuates their crucial role in protecting shorelines, enhancing fishery resources and providing biodiversity value. An impressive array of 170 species of hard corals has been recorded around Pulau Tioman and Pulau Tulai. Reef development is concentrated on the west coast of the island as the east coast is too exposed to tempestuous weather for any coral growth, apart from a few hardy encrusting species and some soft corals.

Some of the best reefs are found around the tiny, dome-shaped island of Pulau Renggis, which is situated off Kampung Lalang. Frigatebirds sometimes roost on this rocky island. Other good reefs are reported south of Tanjung Said on the west coast and at Teluk Elin on the southeast coast. Golden Reef and Tiger Reef boast copious gorgonian sea fans, while the outlying islands such as Pulau Tokong Bahara and Pulau Gut offer the best unspoilt reefs. The rocky outcrop of Pulau Labas off the northwest coast is well known for its splendid multicoloured soft corals. Pulau Tulai, which is a very popular snorkelling spot, has extensive coral reefs that can be found in the main bay in front of the sweeping white sands of Pasir Panjang. This area is characterized by

Location: About 44 km (27 miles) offshore from Mersing, on the southeast coast of Peninsular Malaysia.

Climate: Hot by day, warm by night with sea breezes. There is a single monsoonal period which lasts from about mid-November–mid-January.

When to Go: Between February and October. Sea crossings may continue to be rough until March, and most visitors go from June–September.

Access: From Kuala Lumpur, Kuantan or Singapore by air direct to the island's airport, or by road to Mersing in Johor and thence by ferry to Kampung Tekek on the island's west coast. Boats take between 1½–4 hours, depending on type.

Permits: Not required.

Equipment: Light outdoor clothing and good walking shoes. If you intend to scuba dive, all essential equipment can be rented from companies on the island. For the trek to the peak of Gunung Kajang, camping equipment is required.

Facilities: There is a range of accommodation, from luxurious to cheap. Airport, golf course, clinic. Several dive companies operate on Pulau Tioman.

Watching Wildlife: Reef life off Pulau Renggis, Pulau Chebeh, Tiger Reef, Malang Rock, Pulau Labas. Green turtles mainly May – September, near Kampung Nipah and Pulau Tulai. Birds anywhere at sea, on the coast and in forest. Dolphins and sea snakes are possible out at sea.

Visitor Activities: Snorkelling and scuba diving, swimming, birdwatching, forest trekking. Bicycles can be hired at some resorts. Kampung Lalang offers horse-riding and golf.

Map labels: Pulau Chebeh, Pulau Tulai, Kuala Lumpur, Kg.Salang, Air Batang Bay, Kg.Air Batang, Marine Park Centre, Ferry to Mersing, Kg.Tekek, Pulau Renggis, Kg.Lalang, Kg.Juara, Pulau Tioman, Kg.Genting, Gn.Kajang ▲1040m (3412ft), ▲ Nenek Si Mukut, Kg.Nipah, Kg.Mukut, Pulau Sembilang and Pulau Seri Buat, N

extensive thickets of branching *Acropora* interspersed with narrow gullies of shifting sand.

Swimming, snorkelling and scuba diving are by far the most popular activities in the park. The marine life that rules the deep blue waters is remarkably prolific. Shoals of colourful reef fish including angelfish, rabbitfish, wrasses, fusiliers, snappers, parrotfish and the like are ubiquitous, especially around the Marine Park Centre jetty. They dart frantically amongst the intricate spaces of the reef when the larger groupers and Blacktip Reef Sharks swim by in stately fashion. Both Hawksbill and Green Turtles have been known to nest on Pulau Tioman, although their numbers have declined. The gentle giants of the seas, manta rays and Whale Sharks, have sometimes been sighted in open waters around the islands, especially between the months of March and May.

The resort at Kampung Lalang operates glass-bottomed boat rides to explore the fascinating beauty of Pulau Renggis. Look out for the resident Blacktip Reef Sharks, and the many other fish such as butterflyfish, barracuda, batfish and triggerfish.

Exploring Inland

Picturesque villages dot the island and contribute to its rustic charm. Pulau Tioman has a resident population of over 2,000 people and many local people, traditionally fisherfolk, are now involved directly or indirectly in the lucrative tourism industry.

Many enjoyable activities beckon on land. Head for the jungle-clad hills and scale the spectacular twin gran-

Above: *The social, intelligent cuttlefish use their changing colour patterns for communication; here a male guards a female laying eggs.*

Above: *Clownfish of several species live among the tentacles of sea anemones and are impervious to the anemones' stings.*

Below: *The Hingeback Shrimp is one of the most colourful crustaceans found on the reefs.*

ite peaks. One can, with some persistent enquiry, hire a guide willing to brave the task of climbing the peak of Gunung Kajang. A steep track across the hills connects Kampung Tekek with Kampung Juara, and offers a challenging three-hour trek through tropical forest and bypasses a waterfall cascading down green slopes. Other, shorter treks run between Kampung Air Batang and Kampung Salang, and between Kampung Lalang and Kempung Genting. Alternatively, you can enjoy the tranquil surroundings of the waterfall at Kampung Mukut, site of the famous 'Bali Hai' in the classic 1956 film *South Pacific*.

Right: *The vertical reef wall allows the profuse growth of gorgonian corals.*

Below: *Pulau Tioman's bays provide ideal mooring for fishing boats and tourist craft.*

KRAU WILDLIFE RESERVE

Mammal Research and Study

Set up in 1924, the Krau Wildlife Reserve is the second most important protected area in Peninsular Malaysia after Taman Negara, covering 520 square kilometres (200 square miles). Research on Siamang, the big black gibbon, began in 1968 and many other studies since then have concentrated on White-handed Gibbons, Banded and Dusky Leaf-monkeys, pheasants, mousedeer, macaques, bats and squirrels.

Gunung Benom, the big, lumpy dome of granite that forms the northwest corner of the reserve, is the sixth highest peak in the Peninsula. Krau Wildlife Reserve extends down the eastern and southern slopes of the mountain, reaching the lowlands along the Sungai Krau and Sungai Lompat. It is at the junction of these two rivers that most work has been done, at the research station of Kuala Lompat. The

Department of Wildlife and National Parks maintains a ranger post at Kuala Lompat, and another at Kuala Gandah where the Elephant Translocation Unit is based. Nearby are breeding stations for the *seladang* or Gaur (huge wild cattle), and local deer. The ranger post at Kuala Lompat provides accommodation for researchers working in tall, undisturbed, very productive forest. From here, a network of trails extends through the first few square kilometres of the reserve.

Animal Abundance

In this forest, bordering the two rivers Sungai Krau and Sungai Lompat, the frequently flooding alluvial habitat is rich in big trees of the bean family, which tend to produce edible and nutritious fruits and leaves. These, together with the large number of fig trees, are probably one of the main reasons why monkeys are so abundant.

There used to be some magnificent examples of the big strangling figs with their cathedral-like flying buttress roots – often a sign of previous forest disturbance – and these were common near the rivers because this area used to be settled by Jah Hut people. Most of these people later settled in permanent villages just outside the reserve and the forest around Kuala Lompat was able to recover gradually, with the abundance of fig trees showing where the earlier disturbance had been.

A morning's walk through the forest will almost certainly bring sightings of Banded and Dusky Leaf-monkeys, and of the ubiquitous Long-tailed Macaque. You will surely hear their calls: the banded's rattle, the dusky's donkey-like bray, and the macaque's yapping. White-handed Gibbons and the Siamang, each with a dif-

Opposite, top left: Long-term research has been conducted at Krau on Siamang, the largest of the gibbons.

Opposite, centre left: At Kuala Gandah on the southern boundary, the Che Wong people are one of two main groups using the reserve.

Opposite, bottom left: Small-clawed Otters occur in social groups along the reserve's small rivers.

Opposite, right: Saraca thaipingensis is one of several understorey trees exhibiting cauliflory, or the production of flowers on the trunk.

Above, right: A research station for seladang, *or Gaur, has been set up south of the reserve.*

Climate: Warm by day (hot outside the forest), can be cool by night. A tendency to more rain in April–May and October–January; rivers may flood at any season but more likely December–January.

When to Go: Good at most seasons, but especially February–September, perhaps best for bird-watching April–June.

Access: By road (car, outstation taxi or bus) from Kuala Lumpur towards Temerloh. Turn north towards Jerantut (a change of bus or taxi will be needed in Temerloh), but ask to be deposited at the village of Kuala Krau. Cars can drive direct to base camp at Kuala Lompat; if using public transport, ask for assistance at Kuala Krau.

Permits: Normally open only to serious researchers; a permit must be obtained from the Dept. of Wildlife and National Parks in Kuala Lumpur a few days before you visit.

Equipment: Light clothing, strong walking shoes and a poncho. Take food and other light supplies into the reserve with you (candles, matches, insect repellent are all good ideas). Sleeping bag may be useful.

Facilities: Simple housing available for small numbers, but not suitable for large groups. A good network of trails.

Watching Wildlife: Excellent anywhere along the trails for monkeys and a wide variety of lowland forest birds; gibbons and Siamang mainly in the northwest of trail system. Occasional views of otters and riverine birds at the base camp and in forest.

Visitor Activities: Mainly watching mammals and birds.

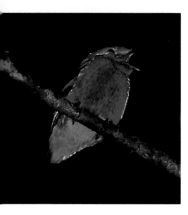

Above: *The frugivorous Green Broadbill is a characteristic forest bird.*

Right: *Research facilities are available at Kuala Lompat for scientists and serious students.*

Below: *Along the trail there is a chance of encountering a flock of Crested Wood Partridges.*

ferent wild whooping duet, may be heard towards the northwest, further away from the base camp.

In addition, there are nocturnal Slow Lorises, civets, wild pigs, deer and mousedeer, tree-rats and the smaller forest cats. Tigers and bears have both been found a little further into the forest, and occasionally come to the research area. Elephants emerge from the forest every few months and may do some damage to cultivation in the nearby villages.

The Forest Bird Community

About 190 species of birds have been recorded so far. Important ones include the Giant Pitta, Malaysian Peacock Pheasant and White-bellied Woodpecker. There is a wide variety of owls and frogmouths, including the Large Frogmouth, a rarity. On the ground are Crested Wood Partridges and Crested Fireback Pheasants, while in the canopy there can be found up to eight species of hornbills, many bulbuls, barbets, pigeons, broadbills, leafbirds, sunbirds – in fact a complete lowland forest bird community.

Gunung Benom

For serious researchers who qualify for access to the reserve, Kuala Lompat is not the only place of interest. One long day is enough to reach the villages of the Che Wong people in the centre of the reserve, and from here at the base of Gunung Benom a trail leads up to the granite outcrop of Batu Gambar Orang.

The peak of Gunung Benom can also be reached from the northeastern boundary of the reserve near Kampung Ulu Cheka. From the summit at 2,107 metres (6,913 feet), on a clear day, Fraser's Hill and the entire Main Range can be seen to the west, and the Peninsula's highest peak, Gunung Tahan in far-off Taman Negara, blue and trembling in the heat-haze.

TAMAN RIMBA KENONG

A Remote Haven for Elephants

Next to Taman Negara, on its southwestern boundary, is Taman Rimba Kenong (Kenong Forest Park). Covering 130 square kilometres (50 square miles) of rare lowland forest, it is important for the conservation of big mammals, especially elephants.

Tree diversity in the park is so great that the amateur cannot hope to identify more than a tiny percentage of those present. Housing thousands of plant species, the forest is a source of many medicinal and nutritious plants ranging from the fruit-bearing wild durians to sugar-yielding palms, cane-producing rattans and the renowned medicinal *Tongkat Ali*.

Wildlife Sightings

Receiving relatively few visitors and lacking a motorable road, Kenong has a sense of remoteness. The chalets and camping sites, though carefully managed, have no electricity supply. Dinner in the evening is lit by candles or carbide lights. The bonus of this isolation is the frequency of wildlife sightings. No guide can promise to show you elephants, which may be present in one place for only a few days at long intervals, but at Kenong your chances of seeing these and other big mammals are better than in most forested areas.

Primates are easily found in Kenong. The commonest of these are Long-tailed Macaques and Dusky Leaf-monkeys, which live in groups inhabiting the limestone hill adjacent to the park's camp. White-handed Gibbons and Banded Leaf-monkeys can often be heard calling, the latter sometimes during the night, while the trek over to the more northerly areas of the park should enable you to hear Siamang, the big black gibbon.

Kenong also holds Sambar Deer, Barking Deer, Gaur (the wild cattle known locally as *seladang*), tapir and bears. Around the camp, Malay Civets and Clouded Monitor Lizards may scavenge for scraps of food, while the Blue Whistling Thrushes that nest on the adjacent limestone can be seen hopping over the ground throughout the day.

Beyond the Base Camp

There is a long trail round the park, which takes from three to five days of trekking. Each night can be spent at one of the beautiful campsites, including the Seven Steps Waterfall and Gunung Putih, the tallest limestone outcrop in the park. The first part of this trek is through particularly good forest over ground that is nearly level, with glimpses of the clear Sungai Kenong to one side. The purity of the water is proved by the abundance of rare aquatic plants that grow in the pebbly river-bed. At several points on the way to the waterfall, the trail crosses the river and the log bridges need negotiating with some care.

In all of these areas beyond the base camp the chances of seeing wildlife are even better. The conspicuous Rhinoceros Hornbill, one of approximately 200 bird species dwelling here, is the pride of the park, usually first detected by the sound of its barking duet. Other

Above, right: Handicrafts are a source of income to villagers at Kampung Kuala Kenong.

Location: Northeast of Kuala Lipis in central Pahang, Kenong is a little way off the Sungai Jelai and abuts the southern boundary of Taman Negara.

Climate: Warm by day, generally warm by night. Scattered rain throughout the year, tending to wet weather in April–May and November–January.

When to Go: Any time of year, but perhaps best around April–June for birds, and August for flowering and fruiting trees.

Access: Kuala Lipis is about 5 hours by road from Kuala Lumpur. By boat from Kuala Lipis jetty to Kampung Kuala Kenong (1 hour), then walk to Kesong Campsite (about 1½ hours). Alternatively by train from Kuala Lipis to Batu Sembilan, then by boat to Kampung Kuala Kenong before walking.

Permits: All visitors must be accompanied by a guide. Arrange your trip through an agent in Kuala Lipis, who will obtain permits from the local office of the State Forestry Department.

Equipment: Light outdoor clothing, with good walking shoes. For caving or climbing, bring your own specialist equipment. Your guide should advise on supplies to be bought in Kuala Lipis before journeying to the park.

Facilities: Chalets at Kesong Campsite, and space for tents. Trails lead to various important locations around the park.

Watching Wildlife: Birdwatching can be good anywhere. Look for signs of large mammals during the walk in, or on the longer trails beyond base camp. Bats and other small wildlife in caves, and a rich array of plant life everywhere.

Visitor Activities: Walking, caving, climbing, wildlife watching.

Above: *Spiral Gingers, named after the way they grow, are sometimes classified in a separate group from other gingers.*

commonly heard hornbill sounds include the groaning of the Black Hornbill, high-pitched yapping from groups of the Bushy-crested Hornbill, and the wild laughter of the Helmeted Hornbill.

Limestone outcrops, rising incongruously amongst the trees, are the park's most distinctive geological structures. Rich in wildlife and rare plants, like many other such hills, they are also rich as a source of legends and ghost stories told by the guides and local villagers. On a trek, perhaps to the northern areas of the park where few visitors have had the opportunity to explore, the combination of white, sculptured limestone and clear little streams within the sunlit forest provide magical scenery. The hills are pitted with caves, some of which can be reached on the trail system leading from the park's headquarters. One, Gua Hijau, is inhabited by a large bat colony. In another, Gua Batu Tangga, a series of rocky ledges forms a natural staircase.

A good trail leads from the base camp all the way round the limestone hill known as Bukit Kesong. This passes through splendid lowland forest giving views of fruit trees, lianas and palms, and passes the entrances to four caves (one accessible by footbridge, and another high up the hillside). An interesting sight during this two- to four-hour trek is a massive wedge of limestone that fell when part of the hill split.

The access trail leading from the perimeter of the park to the base camp makes a pleasant early morning walk. You might see a kingfisher by the riverbank, or ferns and gingers on the forest floor.

Peoples of Kenong

The Batiq people, members of a partly nomadic aboriginal tribe, visit the park at least once a year during the durian fruiting season. Near the park are two Malay villages, and most of the residents are rubber tappers. Elephants cause some problems here, moving through cultivated areas. Various government agencies, together with local organizations including WWF Malaysia, are trying to reduce such conflicts by offering alternative sources of income to the villagers, including handicrafts and involvement in the park's services.

Right: *A series of cascades over limestone make up the Seven Steps Waterfall.*

Far right, top: *The roots of giant fig trees are a help in clambering up the limestone outcrops.*

Far right, bottom: *Small rivers and streams hold rare aquatic plants, while other herbs grow along their banks.*

Opposite: *Efforts are being made to resolve the potential conflicts between man and elephants in and around the park.*

TAMAN NEGARA

Malaysia's First National Park

aman Negara is home to one of the world's oldest tropical rain forests. Plant fossils almost identical with species existing now have been found in rock dating back 130 million years. Established by state legislation in 1938, this was Malaysia's first national park and is the largest, covering 4,343 square kilometres (1,680 square miles). The bulk of the park lies between 75 and 300 metres altitude (250–1,000 feet), fringing the central highland core that rises to the summit of Gunung Tahan, which at 2,187 metres (7,186 feet) is the highest peak in all of Peninsular Malaysia.

Biodiversity

The gently undulating country in the lowlands harbours almost all of the large mammals of Peninsular Malaysia. Most of them will remain invisible, but footprints of tigers, seladang (Gaur), pigs and deer are sometimes found along the walking trails. Elephants may leave evidence of their passage in the form of broken branches in the understorey.

Taman Negara may well contain all of the inland forest bird species that occur in the Peninsula. More than 300 have been counted, of which 292 are known to be dependent on forest for their survival. Another 54 bird

Opposite: *The forest of Taman Negara helps to mitigate flooding along big rivers such as the Sungai Tembeling.*

Above, right: *A range of accommodation is available at the park, including the Taman Negara Resort.*

species are restricted in Taman Negara to highland forest, including two large rarities, the Mountain Peacock Pheasant and the Crested Argus Pheasant.

Though the lowland forest has the greatest variety of plants as well as animals, the highland forest has the most species with very confined distributions. The Tahan massif, for example, is the only known home of *Livistona tahanensis*, an elegant small fan-palm that is quite common there.

Treks and Trails

A walk is the best way to experience the park and its forests, whether it is wandering the well-marked trails around park headquarters at Kuala Tahan, or making longer treks to other areas. In the cool of dawn when birdlife is most active, in the humid sluggishness of midday or the darkness of night, the rain forest offers different impressions. The dense foliage and the retiring habits of the animals mean that most visitors will not at first see much wildlife apart from squirrels, birds and insects. But if one is very quiet, it will not be long before other inhabitants such as monkeys, gibbons and perhaps even a mousedeer will appear.

The 400-metre (1,300-foot) canopy walkway at Kuala Tahan, the longest such walkway in the world, gives birdwatchers many opportunities. Those seeking bigger animals, such as deer or tapir, may try their luck by staying overnight at a hide overlooking a salt lick or clearing, such as Yong Hide, Blau Hide or, best of all, Kumbang Hide. The self-discipline to keep very still is needed when

Location: Spreads over areas of Pahang, Kelantan and Terengganu; 59 km (37 miles) upriver from Kuala Tembeling, which is 54 km (34 miles) north of Temerloh on the Kuala Lumpur-to-Kuantan road.

Climate: 25°–37°C (77°–99°F). Typically hot and humid, but cool and sunny in mountains, cold on peaks at night. More rain expected October–February.

When to Go: Best March–September, less favourable for walking and viewing wildlife from mid-November–mid-January.

Access: Taxi or train to Kuala Tembeling on the Singapore-to-Kota Bharu line. Or bus to Jerantut then taxi to Tembeling. Boat up the Sungai Tembeling to park HQ. Now possible to drive or fly direct to a point near Kuala Tahan. Alternative access points in Kelantan and Terengganu.

Permits: Bookings for park boats and accommodation are made with agents such as Taman Negara Resort office in Kuala Lumpur, but shop around for other operators or ask at Kuala Tahan. Entry, camera and fishing fees payable at park HQ.

Equipment: Hiking, camping and fishing equipment available for hire at the park. Take torch for night walks. Light clothing for forest use, warm clothes if intending to climb; walking boots and sleeping bag for serious hiking.

Facilities: Reception and information centre, chalets, camping area, restaurants and shop. Three visitors' lodges and two fishing lodges. Hides and extensive canopy walkway.

Watching Wildlife: Excellent birdwatching in all areas of the park. Bats and snakes in various caves. Possibly elephants, bears and other big mammals.

Visitor Activities: Walking and trekking, river trips, swimming, watching wildlife.

Above: *Fungi are little studied but of huge importance in nutrient cycling within the forest.*

you are on lookout. Large animals may not come every night but these hides are the best, though not guaranteed, means of seeing them.

Guides are required for longer treks, which include interesting trips to some of the lime-stone caves found in Taman Negara. The most often visited cave is Gua Telinga, less than an hour's walk south of Kuala Tahan. Gua Daun Menari is larger, with more bats, accessible from Kuala Keniyam. Gua Besar is a limestone massif still deeper into the forest, but with few caves. Gua Peningat, highest limestone peak in the peninsula at 714 metres (2,340 feet), is reached via the western access point of Merapoh, and energetic visitors can scramble all the way up to the top.

Climbing Gunung Tahan

Those with more time can attempt the ascent of Gunung Tahan. At least seven days of trekking are needed to cover the 55 kilometres (35 miles) from Kuala Tahan and back again. The second day is the most gruelling, and involves a climb up and down 21 hills. On the third day the climb of the mountain really begins, part of it on all fours up earth banks, before emerging at mid-mountain altitude at Wray's Camp. The last day includes a scramble up steep quartzite, and ends at the famous *padang* of low, open scrub just below the true peak. Here you may see the Hill Prinia, a small warbler-like bird for which the *padang* is its only home between northern Thailand and Sumatra. An ascent from Merapoh can shorten the trek to three days.

Rivers and Rapids

A less strenuous but more expensive way to explore the natural features of Taman Negara is to hire a boat for a trip along one of the park's many rivers and tributaries. These include a scenic ride to the rapids of Lata Berkoh and a journey through

Right: *Leaf-insects, magnificently coloured to resemble growing leaves, are active mainly by night.*

Far right: *Each red lobe of the ginger inflorescence represents one flower.*

Below, right: *Water monitors can be seen by most visitors along the rivers or even at the headquarters of the park.*

Opposite, left: *Aboriginal peoples, though they have carefully defined rights within the park, now depend little upon hunting.*

Opposite, right: *Taman Negara has the longest canopy walkway anywhere in the world.*

the whitewater rapids of the Sungai Tembeling. Boat trips can also shorten the treks to some of the less accessible places within the park, which include Kuala Terengan and Kuala Keniyam and the wildlife observation hides.

Access and Accommodation

Taman Negara now has four access points: Kuala Tahan and Merapoh in Pahang, Kuala Koh in Kelantan, and Tanjung Mentong in Terengganu. Kuala Tahan, the traditional entry point into the park, is accessible by boat (a three hour ride) from Kuala Tembeling near Jerantut in Pahang; or by air from Kuala Lumpur and Singapore. Merapoh can be reached by ordinary car or by train, Kuala Koh by four-wheel drive along jeep tracks through the oil-palm plantations. Access to the newest visitor centre at Tanjung Mentong, in Terengganu, is only by boat across Kenyir lake. This centre is notable for two features: it is within reach of the limestone hills Gua Bidan and Gua Taat, and also offers the possibility of a trek to the little-known mountain Gunung Gagau. Accommodation within the park includes a hostel, chalets and campsites.

Above, top: *The ascent of Gunung Tahan, the Peninsula's highest mountain, involves a trek of several days.*

Above, centre: *Fishing is permitted in certain areas, but only with a licence.*

Above, bottom: *The challenge of the rapids alters from day to day, depending on water levels.*

Right: *Trees arching over the smaller rivers are a special feature of the lowland forest here.*

ULU KELANTAN

Limestone Hills and River Rapids

U lu Kelantan is an informal name for the south-ern, and once very remote, region of the state of Kelantan. Though now opened up by roads and planted with newly developed rubber and oil palm plantations, the area is still sparsely populated. Nature is a prime asset. Much of Ulu Kelantan is still covered in forest, and a quarter of Taman Negara is situated there.

Gunung Stong

Among the unique attractions of Ulu Kelantan is the magnificent Stong Waterfall, flowing from the three adjacent peaks of Gunung Stong, Gunung Ayam and Gunung Saji. The waterfall is possibly the highest and certainly the most spectacular in Peninsular Malaysia. It cascades down sheer granite walls, and can be seen from many kilometres away. Until recently, Stong Waterfall was unheard of due to its difficult access. Today, with the completion of the road from Jeli to Dabong, it is much easier to reach.

Information about the flora and fauna of Gunung Stong is scarce. There are two small, pretty endemic herbs found only on this mountain, and sphagnum moss, sedges, pitcher plants and conifers grow near the peaks.

Opposite: The granite slopes of Gunung Stong Waterfall are stripped of soil and vegetation by their steepness and by water flow.

Above, right: The Blue Bottle can be seen, settled with groups of other butterflies, at natural water seepages.

Wild bananas and gingers are abundant on the middle levels of the mountain. Tracks and droppings of elephants, tiger, tapir and deer can be expected here, and elephants may be standing silent and uncomfortably close to the trail. Locally based guides should be able to keep you safe and on the right path.

Ulu Kelantan Limestone

Kelantan has more limestone hills than any other state in Malaysia, over 200 of them, nearly all situated in the south. Particularly impressive massifs are found around the town of Gua Musang, along the Sungai Nenggiri, and beside the railway through Ulu Kelantan.

Many of the hills contain caves. Gua Renayang, near the aboriginal resettlement scheme at Kuala Betis, west of Gua Musang, has a high cave with a chimney to the top of the hill, and a deep trough in the floor where the river can be heard flowing. Within the town boundary of Gua Musang, the hill of the same name has a huge cave. Excavations in the 1930s revealed that parts of it had been used as a pottery workshop and kiln site during the palaeolithic period.

Cave entrances provide shelter for many animals, including elephants, Serow, deer, various rodents, and birds like peregrine falcons, swifts and swallows. Blue Rock Thrush, Blue Whistling Thrush and Crag Martin are amongst the birds that specialize on the limestone habitat. Of great interest are the 'living' caves that support many bats. The cave fruit bat that roosts in the lighter parts of caves is a main pollinator of durian trees.

Location: Ulu Kelantan is a broad swathe of country, the southern two-thirds of Kelantan, the Peninsula's most northeasterly state.

Climate: Generally hot, with warm nights, and usually a strongly marked wet season around November–January.

When to Go: Best between about March–September, but possible at any time. Floods can interfere with travel especially around November–January.

Access: Overland by road to Gua Musang, from the south via Kuala Lipis, or from the north via Kota Bharu and Kuala Krai. A main train line runs through from Kuala Lipis to Kota Bharu and Tumpat. A car or 4-wheel drive vehicle is a great advantage.

Permits: Not generally required, except to enter forest areas when permits should be obtained from the Forest Office in the nearest large town.

Equipment: Light clothing and good walking shoes suitable for forest use. Bring a poncho. Little equipment available on the spot, so bring your own for camping, caving, etc.

Facilities: For local transport use trains, or arrange with residents to share a lorry, car or motorcycle. Local towns offer budget accommodation, eating places and shops for varied supplies. Some better known sites (e.g. Gunung Stong) have developed facilities with guides.

Watching Wildlife: Find a competent guide to take you to forested areas. Wide range of wildlife of all sizes. Along Sungai Nenggiri, saltlicks and signs of elephants and Gaur. Good birdwatching almost anywhere in forest or forest edge.

Visitor Activities: Trekking, camping, boating and rafting, climbing, wildlife watching. Caving in many limestone areas.

Right: *The Sungai Nenggiri formed a major travel and trade route through the Ulu Kelantan region in earlier centuries.*

Above: *Reticulated Pythons are hard to find; the smaller individuals are considered harmless.*

Right: *Crafts practised in the rural areas include both the ancient, such as blowpipe manufacture, and the modern, such as the use of dyes on mats.*

River Trips into History

An outdoor activity not to be missed when visiting Ulu Kelantan is a trip down the Sungai Nenggiri, either by raft, canoe or longboat. In the distant past the river, which has its source near the Kelantan–Perak border north of Cameron Highlands, was an important trading and migration route. Spectacular limestone outcrops, some with caves inhabited by man in the distant past, line the river. At Gua Cha evidence of neolithic burials makes this one of the most important archaeological sites in the Peninsula. Further down the river, you can stop at Gua Jaya (or Gua Yahaya) and Gua Cawan, two other caves known for their prehistory. Here, excavations have revealed burial sites, animal bones from ancient meals, pottery fragments and stone tools.

Sungai Nenggiri can be physically challenging even for the most experienced boatman. Far upstream is the very dangerous rapid known as Jeram Gajah (Elephant Rapids), where a single rock lies right at the centre of the whitewater exit and local boatmen rightly refuse to carry any passengers through. However, on boat trips from Kuala Betis it is possible to experience some of the safer rapids such as Jeram Kalong and Jeram Batu.

Other Journeys

Ulu Kelantan is so big that the range of possibilities for the visitor is almost unlimited. A fascinating journey on land and river can be made between Cameron Highlands and Gua Musang. Beginning at the Blue Valley Tea Estate at nearly 1,200 metres (4,000 feet), you can pass from village to village, through forest and cultivation, before reaching the Sungai Nenggiri for an exhilarating rafting trip downstream.

The village of Blau is a good centre from which to reach the mountain of Gunung Ayam (several peaks in Kelantan share this name) as well as to take river and caving trips. Dabong is a small town on the railway which can also serve as a holiday base.

A new opportunity has arisen with the opening of visitor facilities on the Kelantan side of Taman Negara. Reached via estate roads from Gua Musang, a four-wheel drive may be needed to get there, but it is worth the effort. A pleasing river runs nearby, good birdwatching is available, and bears, among other exciting wildlife, have been seen close to the chalets.

Above: *A trip along the Sungai Nenggiri will include both calm and whitewater stretches.*

SETIU

Wetlands and Seashore Habitats

Setiu is the second northernmost district in the idyllic east coast state of Terengganu. It is well known for its beautiful continuous stretch of light brown sun-soaked sandy beach, from Kampung Merang in the south to Beting Lintang in the north. The small rivers of the Setiu-Chalok-Bari Basin form a wetland of national and international significance, with a catchment of about 230 square kilometres (89 square miles).

The Sungai Setiu flows from the Gunung Tebu Forest Reserve, a steep forested area covering the mountain range from Gunung Tebu (1,037 metres/3,402 feet) to Gunung Lawit (1,518 metres/4,980 feet). A unique feature of the river is the extensive brackish-water estuary which is scattered with sandy islands.

Coconut and casuarina are the common trees along the coast. Mangrove forests, dominated by trees such as *Sonneratia* and *Rhizophora*, and riparian forest line the Setiu and most of its tributaries. Further inland, cashew nut trees are common and gelam trees, *Melaleuca cajeputi*, with their distinctive flaky bark, grow abundantly.

Opposite: Setiu's sandy, tropical beaches remain for the moment unspoilt and undeveloped; facilities for visitors are few and there is only simple beach hut accommodation. Behind the palm-fringed beaches, the favoured nesting site of several species of marine turtles, sand deposition has formed an extensive system of lagoons and inlets which are rich in birdlife.

Above, right: The White-throated Kingfisher is common in all open habitats, from the coast inland.

SOUTH CHINA SEA
Kg.Beting Lintang
Kuala Setiu Baharu
Kuala Lumpur
Kg.Penarik
Besut
S.Setiu
Kg.Bari
Kg.Merang
Kg.Buloh
N
Setiu
Batu Rakit
Kuala Terengganu
Tekah

Animal Life

At least 29 species of mammals, 112 species of birds, and 28 species of reptiles have been recorded in the area, inhabiting a diverse array of microhabitats. Tigers and bears are some of the large mammals that have been seen in the gelam forest. Bird species that are characteristic of Peninsular Malaysia's east coast, and unlikely to be seen elsewhere, include the Red-wattled Lapwing, Lineated Barbet and Indian Roller.

Along the Sungai Setiu or Sungai Chalok, Smooth Otters, large Water Monitor Lizards, troops of Long-tailed Macaques, and many species of kingfishers, tailorbirds, sunbirds, malkohas and pigeons may be seen in a single morning. A night cruise may be rewarded by sightings of civets, owls, snakes, flying foxes, wild pigs or even estuarine crocodiles. At night fireflies can also be seen in large aggregations on the *Sonneratia* and *Gluta* trees, brightening up the river bank with their bioluminescence.

Turtles and Terrapins

Setiu is well known for its marine turtles and is one of several major rookeries for Green Turtles, and for the smallest species of marine turtle in the world, the Olive Ridley. The giant Leatherback nests here occasionally.

Sungai Setiu is home to possibly the largest population of Painted Terrapins, known locally as *tuntung laut*, anywhere in the world. These hard-shelled, fully aquatic, freshwater turtles are restricted to Southeast Asia and their numbers have declined throughout their range. During the mating season, the adult males, much smaller than their female partners, undergo a dramatic colour

Location: On the sandy coast of Terengganu in the northeast, 60 km (38 miles) north of Kuala Terengganu.

Climate: Hot to stifling by day, warm to hot by night, with sea breezes. Dry for much of the year, with a marked wet period usually about October–February.

When to Go: Best between March–September, with turtles mainly May onwards; any time of year possible if you are willing to face flooding in wet season.

Access: By bus or taxi from Kuala Terengganu, along the old coastal road via Kampung Merang.

Permits: Not required, except for watching nesting turtles and terrapins (apply to the Department of Fisheries).

Equipment: Wear light clothing, a wide-brimmed hat to keep off the sun, and sunblock cream. Swimming gear, and a poncho for wet weather. A torch is useful.

Facilities: Beach chalets are available at Bari and Setiu, and some villagers here and at Penarik are willing to arrange homestay accommodation. Few eating shops. There are no other facilities, but a resort development is under consideration. Away from Setiu there is a small resthouse at Kuala Merang and other small holiday businesses here and further south.

Watching Wildlife: Turtle watching at night. Birdwatching is excellent along the shore, in mangrove fragments and vegetation further inland.

Visitor Activities: Turtle watching, birdwatching, boating on lagoon and river to look for terrapins, monitor lizards and other wildlife. Swimming, camping and walking, paying due regard to local land ownership.

Above: *The lagoons at Setiu contain some brackish-water palms,* Nypa fruticans.

transformation. The head turns from dull grey with a dull orange stripe between the eyes, to white with a bright scarlet stripe. Even the shell becomes lighter and brighter with numerous contrasting black patches. During the nesting season adult females swim out to sea and along the coast to lay their elongated eggs in pits dug on the sandy beaches.

Turtle and terrapin watching can be very interesting, but these shy creatures are easily frightened by noise, bright lights and human movement on the beach, and may abort nesting. Visitors should follow the advice of local villagers, and avoid causing disturbance with lights or camera flashes. The nesting season of marine turtles and terrapins peaks between June and August. The eggs are harvested by licensed egg collectors, and visitors intending to observe these reptiles nesting at Setiu should seek permission from the Department of Fisheries. WWF Malaysia and the Department of Fisheries have for many years studied the nesting ecology of marine turtles and of Painted Terrapins at Setiu in order to conserve them.

Above: *The Setiu beaches have been identified as important nesting sites for the Olive Ridley Turtle.*

New Proposals

It has been proposed to the state government that the coastal and wetland areas around Sungai Setiu should be established as a state park. The proposed boundaries include an area of approximately 150 square kilometres (58 square miles) of land, plus a strip of sea 3.68 kilometres (2 nautical miles) wide along the coast from Telaga Papan to Beting Lintang. Such a park would need to accommodate the economic and development aspirations of the local residents but its establishment would ensure that the beauty and wilderness of Setiu could be preserved for many years to come.

Above: *Coconut palms form a major feature of the landscape on Setiu's attractive coastal plains.*

Left: *Green Turtles are shy creatures and easily disturbed when nesting.*

PULAU REDANG MARINE PARK

Prolific Reef Life in Azure Waters

The Pulau Redang Marine Park is situated about 45 kilometres (28 miles) northeast of Kuala Terengganu, the sleepy capital of the state of Terengganu. The marine park comprises the waters off nine islands, which are in several natural groups. These are the Redang group; the Perhentian group; Pulau Lang Tengah, which lies halfway between these two groups, and Pulau Kapas which is 64 kilometres (40 miles) to the south and much closer inshore. Most visitors go to one of the main islands, either Pulau Redang or Pulau Perhentian, the latter being the less visited destination.

The Pulau Redang Group
Pulau Redang, Pulau Pinang, Pulau Lima and the six islets off Redang's eastern and southern shores make up the Pulau Redang group of islands. The little islets are called Pulau Paku Besar, Pulau Paku Kecil, Pulau Ekor Tebu, Pulau Kerengga Besar, Pulau Kerengga Kecil and

Opposite, top left: *Shaped like a purple dragon, the sea slug* Flabellina rubrolineata *wends slowly over the reef.*

Opposite, bottom left: *Soft corals such as* Dendronephthya hemprichi *sway with every slight change in the water current, and are easily damaged by trampling.*

Opposite, right: *A big table coral like this* Acropora *is a colony containing millions of individual polyps.*

Above, right: *Diving is increasingly popular with both Malaysians and foreign visitors.*

Pulau Ling. They are just half an hour's speedboat ride from the mainland coastal village of Kampung Merang (not to be confused with the town of Marang).

Pulau Redang itself is about 25 square kilometres (9½ square miles) in area. It is dominated by two imposing north-south ridges separated by a low-lying central valley. The coast on the eastern side of the island is blessed with sweeping, white sandy beaches, while the western side is wilder, more rocky in nature. The vegetation on the island is lush, characterized by varied forest types. A resident population of over 1,000 people lives in the village of Kampung Redang, which is situated at the estuary of the river and housed entirely on stilts over the sea. Fishing and related cottage-based industries form the economic foundation for most villagers, although many are now also involved in tourism-related activities and can provide boats.

Redang's Coral Reefs
In the azure waters surrounding the island and its satellites are probably the best reefs found off Peninsular Malaysia, with hard and soft corals of every hue and shape supporting a very high diversity of associated marine flora and fauna.

The reefs here extend from sea level down to 20 metres (66 feet). There is some coral off the east coast, in areas sheltered from the direct wrath of storms, but the most extensive development is around the smaller islets. The northern and eastern sides of the islets especially, which are characterized by deeper waters, have a

Map labels: Pulau Rawa, Pulau Susu Dara, Pulau Perhentian Kecil, Pulau Perhentian Besar, Kuala Besut, Pulau Lang Tengah, Pulau Redang, Pulau Lima, Pulau Pinang, Pulau Ekor Tebu, Pulau Bidong Laut, Kg.Penarik, Kg.Merang, Kuala Terengganu, Marang, Pulau Kapas, Kuala Lumpur, Pulau Redang Marine Park, N

Above: *Longnosed Filefish
pick food particles from
between the corals.*

Below right: *Pasir Panjang
is one of several secluded
beaches on Pulau Redang.*

more diverse coral fauna. A variety of marine habitats can be found, including shallow coral areas, shallow rock faces, moderate depth slopes and cliffs with little grottoes. Abundant shallow reef flats and coral gardens are dominated by the branching corals *Acropora* and *Montipora*. In waters between about 10 and 20 metres (33–66 feet), extensive areas of soft corals, *Porites* and *Fungia*, brain corals and barrel sponges take one's breath away. Still deeper areas are well characterized by *Dendrophyllia, Tubastrea*, sea whips and sea fans. Large coral boulders are present in many places. At Pulau Ling there is one colossal *Porites* coral boulder, approximately 40 metres (130 feet) in circumference and 10 metres (33 feet) high, with a cave at its base. In places where the cliffs are steep, colourful soft and encrusting corals and sea anemones carpet the granite. Of special interest are the eastern slopes of Pulau Pinang, where the biggest stand of blue corals, *Helipora coerulea*, known in Malaysia is found.

Reef fish and pelagics are plentiful, with parrotfish, damselfish, wrasses and triggerfish darting between the corals, or surrounding you at the jetty at the Marine Park Centre. Occasionally a manta ray or a Whale Shark may be seen in the open waters within and around the park. Pulau Redang also has the largest breeding populations of Green and Hawksbill Turtles in Terengganu.

Popular dive sites include the Big Seamount, Pulau Lima, Terumbu Kili, Mini Seamount and Pulau Ekor Tebu. The reef in front of the Marine Park Centre on Pulau Pinang is also worth a trip, especially for snorkellers.

The Pulau Perhentian Group

The Pulau Perhentian group of islands comprises Pulau Perhentian Besar, Pulau Perhentian Kecil, Pulau Susu Dara and several smaller islets to the northwest. Situated 20 kilometres (12 miles) off the coast near the town of Kuala Besut in Terengganu, the islands are easily accessible by boat and offer an unspoilt paradise for visitors, with uncrowded white beaches that slope gently down to coral reefs in pure blue water.

Above: *The brightly
marked Coral Grouper
typically stays close to
the reef.*

Below: *Some parrotfish
species have brilliant
peacock colouring.*

Pulau Perhentian Besar, the largest of the three main islands, covers 950 hectares (2,345 acres). Pulau Perhentian Kecil, about two-thirds the size, is separated from it by a wide sandy channel which contains scattered corals, with seagrass patches in the deeper areas. Fringing coral reefs are mainly concentrated off the bays and coves. The islets are primarily jumbles of huge volcanic boulders, tumbling down to a depth of 30 metres (100 feet), forming caves, crevices and tunnels.

In the clear waters various pelagic fishes abound, including jacks, trevallies and barracuda. Most of the smaller angelfish, pufferfish, filefish, triggerfish, boxfish, batfish, lionfish, scorpionfish, cardinalfish, hawkfish, breams and coral trout can be seen. Usually something colourful and different appears on every dive. Octopus, cuttlefish and squid can also be found. Two species of turtles, Green and Hawksbill, are reported to come ashore regularly to lay their eggs.

Right: *Diverse forms of marine life, including impressive red featherstars, can be seen on Pulau Perhentian's coral reefs.*

SARAWAK

S arawak is the biggest of Malaysia's 13 states, with a land area of 124,658 square kilometres (48,130 square miles) occupying the northern quarter of the island of Borneo. It is almost as big as all eleven states of Peninsular Malaysia taken together, and about two-thirds of it is covered in forest. The coastline extends for 1,035 kilometres (640 miles).

The state is noted for the number and size of its parks. There are now ten national parks, and several wildlife sanctuaries, wildlife centres and nature reserves. Those open to the public range from the small to the vast, and an itinerary can include anything from an easy day-trip to a challenging expedition. Each national park has some special feature. Bako and Gunung Mulu, for example, both have spectacular rock formations, one of sandstone, the other of limestone cliffs and caves, yet they offer incomparable contrasts. Gunung Gading protects *Rafflesia*, and Loagan Bunut a way of life based on fishing. Within Niah is the most famous archaeological site in Southeast Asia. There is, therefore, a feeling of a planned network, within which each park is fulfilling a particular conservation function.

Instead of relying on roads, travel to Sarawak's exciting places often begins by air, followed by river journeys past forest-lined banks. Depending on location, these rivers may be giant, slow-moving waterways, tranquil forest streams, whitewater rapids or shallow pebbled beds over which boats must be hauled. Beside the waters, traditional longhouse dwellings can still be found, some of which can be visited by arrangement.

In Sarawak, one seldom sees the progressive altitudinal zona-tion of forest types that characterizes the Peninsula. The forest is influenced more by subtle differences in soil and drainage than it is by height above sea level. Sarawak is special in having big areas of peat swamp forest on the coastal plains, and in hav-ing strange heath forest on areas of poor soils. It is special, too, for the presence of oxbow lakes, and the fantastically high plant diversity encountered within some of its protected areas.

TANJUNG DATU NATIONAL PARK

Sarawak's Westernmost Cape

Gazetted in 1994, Tanjung Datu forms one of Sarawak's newer and smaller parks, containing about 14 square kilometres (5 square miles) of rather unusual forest. Its value for nature conservation is greatly enhanced by the fact that it is very close to Samunsam Wildlife Sanctuary, covering another 60 square kilometres (23 square miles).

Tanjung Datu is a long cape, pointing north, with a lighthouse at the tip and with a hilly interior that is neatly divided by the international border between Malaysia and Indonesia. The highest point in the park, Gunung Melanau, at 543 metres (1,781 feet), is on the border.

A Forest Mosaic

Perhaps most important for wildlife in this area is the mosaic of different forest types, patchily intermixed because of small differences in soil and drainage. Most of the park is on fragile and nutrient-poor soils that are not suited for timber production or for any form of shifting or settled agriculture. In parts of Sarawak where

Opposite: *Silvered Leaf monkeys are found mainly in coastal and riverine forest.*

Above, right: *Easy to walk through, the forest contains a vast structural array of climbers, herbs, trees, lianas and epiphytes of many species.*

Previous pages
Page 82: *Deep in the forest near Batang Ai National Park, a traditionally tattooed Iban rests in his dug out.*
Page 83: *The Rhinoceros Hornbill: the spectacular natural inspiration for culture and art in Sarawak.*

these conditions are most extreme, such forest is known as *kerangas*, an Iban word describing sandy areas where crops will not flourish.

In Tanjung Datu, mixed dipterocarp forest and heath forest (*kerangas*) can be seen in varied combinations, while the shoreline bears another range of plants adapted to the special conditions there. One of these is the tree *Barringtonia asiatica*, or Putat, which produces scented pink and white powder-puff flowers as big as a tennis ball; they open at night and are pollinated by moths and probably also by bats. The fallen blooms can be found along the sandy shore in the morning. The Putat flower is the park's emblem. On the sand at the top of the beach is the Sea Morning Glory *Ipomoea pes-caprae*, a mauve-flowered creeper with leaves shaped like a goat's hoof.

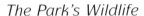

The Park's Wildlife

Within the subtle and complex forest patchwork of Tanjung Datu live many interesting birds and mammals. High on the wish list of any birdwatcher is the colourful but elusive Bornean Bristlehead, a bird endemic to Borneo. Small groups of Bristleheads may pass noiselessly through the canopy, or linger within the middle layers of the forest to search for cicadas and katydids.

There are other important birds, too, in other habitats. The Hook-billed Bulbul, a Borneo endemic, is fairly common in the heath forest. Storm's Stork, internationally threatened, occurs in small numbers and is more likely to be seen in the riverside trees along the Sungai Samunsam than within the boundaries of Tanjung Datu. The rare Malaysian Plover, a bird of sandy and pebble

Location: The westernmost cape on the coast of Sarawak, next to the Kalimantan border. It is adjacent to Samunsam Wildlife Sanctuary.

Climate: Hot by day but comfortable within the forest (average about 32°C/90°F) and warm by night. Sea breezes.

When to Go: March–September are better for sea crossings to the park; in the rougher, wet and windy weather commoner from October–February it may be inaccessible. December and January typically the wettest months, May–July may be the driest.

Access: Overland, most easily by hired car or taxi but more cheaply by bus, from Kuching via Bau and Lundu to Sematan. By boat from there to the park.

Permits: Should be arranged with the National Parks and Wildlife Office in Kuching before departure. Permission to visit Samunsam Wildlife Sanctuary is always limited to researchers.

Equipment: Light clothing for beach and forest walking, and protection from the sun. As facilities at Tanjung Datu are still under development, camping equipment, food and cooking equipment should be brought.

Facilities: At present few facilities are in place. Most recent information should be sought from the National Parks and Wildlife Office, Kuching.

Watching Wildlife: An important site for primates (including gibbons, Silvered Leaf-monkeys) and coastal wildlife. Occasional seabirds, migrants, Malaysian Plover along the shore. Forest bird community includes rare Bornean Bristleheads and the Hook-billed Bulbul. Porpoises may be spotted at sea.

Visitor Activities: Birdwatching in the forest, forest edge and along the coast, beach fossicking, walking, camping and swimming.

Above: *Western Tarsiers jump from sapling to sapling in the understorey, looking for big insects.*

Above, right: *The Slow Loris, not always slow-moving, is best found at night by using a headlamp.*

Right: *The white-tipped female Rajah Brooke Birdwing (above) is much more rarely seen than the male (below).*

shores, is a proven breeder here. The sight of an adult trotting in front of somebody walking along the beach is a warning not to trample a well-camouflaged egg or chick. This plover is very vulnerable to disturbance, so the relatively peaceful Tanjung Datu beaches are therefore valuable in maintaining at least a scattered chain of sites where it can breed.

Five primates are active by day in the forests of Tanjung Datu: Long-tailed and Pig-tailed Macaques, Banded and Silvered Leaf-monkeys, and the Bornean Gibbon. Two more, the Slow Loris and the Tarsier, are nocturnal. The large eyes of the Tarsier do not reflect torchlight, which is unusual in animals that are active after dark. Although this tiny creature is hard to spot, you may hear its high-pitched calls as it forages in the trees.

Special Features

Plants of particular interest to visitors to Tanjung Datu, because of their unusual appearance, include pitcher plants and the umbrella palm *Johannesteysmannia*

altifrons. The huge leaves of this understorey palm are outstanding in both their size and beauty.

Tanjung Datu has several other features that are of special interest. It is perhaps the only place in Sarawak where clear streams drain directly down from the mountains to the sea; everywhere else, a broad coastal plain intervenes. The beach at Labuhan Gadong is a turtle nesting area, and a turtle hatchery has been established at the park.

Samunsam Wildlife Sanctuary, 20 minutes away by boat, is open only to researchers. Here, plant diversity is much higher in the riverine forest than in the nearby mangroves, and plant productivity is also more seasonal, which affects the appearance of primates such as the Proboscis Monkey. In the mixed dipterocarp, heath and secondary forest, the existence of so many primates at one site makes a complex picture of interactions between the animals and their habitat, mediated by soil, food supply and climate.

GUNUNG GADING NATIONAL PARK

Conserving the World's Largest Flower

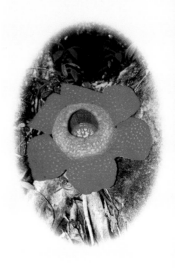

In the everwet tropics, where species diversity is enormous, it is rare to have a big reserve established for a single species. Perhaps the closest approach to this in Malaysia is in Sarawak where, in addition to sanctuaries created for the protection of Orang-utans and Proboscis Monkeys, Gunung Gading National Park was set up in large part to protect a population of the spectacular plant *Rafflesia tuan-mudae*.

Established in 1983, the park contains 41 square kilometres (16 square miles) of hilly mixed dipterocarp forest. Gunung Gading itself is an isolated, conical peak near the coast, reaching 906 metres (2,946 feet).

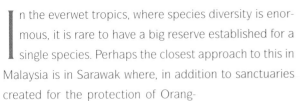

The Giant Rafflesia

Lower down, the forest is fine and tall, and interspersed with small streams. In places the understorey is a tangle of vines, climbing plants in the genus *Tetrastigma*. These vines, members of the grape family, are important as hosts to the magnificent, parasitic *Rafflesia*. At Gunung Gading, buds of *Rafflesia* can be found nearly all year round. A bud begins as a small excrescence on the looping woody stem of its host, nearly always at ground level where the vine stem runs along the earth or under the leaf litter. For many weeks this hard, round, heavy growth becomes gradually bigger, like a slowly swelling cabbage, with a surface that is increasingly rosy in colour and shiny in texture.

The time of opening can be predicted a day or two in advance, as the outer lobes of the flower begin to lift. Real enthusiasts have been known to camp out overnight in order to catch every stage of the flowering on film, and

it is said that during the opening there is an audible pop.

The biology of *Rafflesia* is very poorly known. It has not yet been grown in botanical gardens, and efforts in various parts of Southeast Asia to create new colonies in the wild (by placing apparently ripe seeds on the host vines) have not been successful.

Like most of its relatives, *Rafflesia tuan-mudae* is thought to have a very restricted distribution, being found only in Sarawak. However, it is closely related to plants bearing other names (*Rafflesia arnoldii* in Sumatra, and *R. keithii* in Sabah) and these may all be members of a single species. The whole group includes the biggest flowers in the world. There is a lot of size variation between blooms even at one locality, probably related to the amount of nutrients the parasite is able to gather from its host before flowering. At Gunung Gading, the biggest examples of *Rafflesia* reach about one metre (3 feet) across; they are orange-red, with small whitish raised blobs all over the open flower surface.

Visitors to Gunung Gading are most likely to see buds. The open flowers each last only a few days, but with luck an advance telephone call to the park staff may bring the welcome news of a bud about to open. If so, then a trip to the park will enable you to see, and smell, something unique, for the open flower has a mild scent attractive to flies and other insect pollinators.

Much damage to these plants can be caused by trampling. At Gunung Gading, a good plankwalk with

Above, right: Rafflesias normally have five petals. Finding a six petalled example such as this is almost unheard of.

Location: An isolated mountain west of the small town of Lundu, 60 km (37 miles) west of the state capital of Kuching.

Climate: Equable temperatures within the forest; can be cool at night, especially at higher elevations on the mountain.

When to Go: Any time of year is suitable, but neither wet weather nor *Rafflesia* blooms can be predicted with certainty.

Access: Simple, about 2 hours by road from Kuching via Bau to Lundu. The park is a few minutes from Lundu town.

Permits: Arranged with staff of the National Parks and Wildlife Office, at the park headquarters.

Equipment: No special equipment needed; light clothing, walking shoes, swimming gear and a towel. Camera and film suitable for low light conditions, to photograph plants.

Facilities: Walking trails and swimming spots, accommodation and an interpretation and information centre. Other facilities are available in nearby Lundu.

Watching Wildlife: Not much animal life, the park is important for *Rafflesia* as well as being a popular recreational site for foreign and domestic tourists. Good chance of seeing the widespread but seldom-flowering plant *Amorphophallus*, a giant aroid lily.

Visitor Activities: Primarily the chance to look for the *Rafflesia* flower and other rare plants, with photography; swimming, walking, trekking. Visitors must take care to avoid trampling *Rafflesia* buds. Beaches at Pandan and Siar are easily accessible from Lundu.

Right: *The fully open
Rafflesia flower is a star-
tling find during a walk
through the forest.*

Above: *The rarely flowering
aroid Amorphophallus is
unusually common at
Gunung Gading.*

handrails has been built past the main *Rafflesia* sites, so that damage to the flowers is prevented.

Forest Walks

Gunung Gading is a landmark visible throughout the area of Lundu, the nearest town. The Sungai Lundu is the main river draining the park, and in its upper stretches it has several attractive small waterfalls. Flowing between smoothly rounded boulders, the clear water is very invit- ing and accounts for the many local visitors who come to the park, especially at weekends. There are marked jun-

gle trails to explore leading through the rocky forest, and if no *Rafflesia* happen to be in flower then there may be other unusual plants to see, such as *Amorphophallus*, another giant, which is a member of the aroid lily family.

The Waterfall Trail is quite an easy walk along a well- marked route. The water in the stream is cool and clear, coming directly from the mountain. It is also possible to climb to the peak of Gunung Gading. This is a steep and arduous trek which requires permission from the park staff and the services of a guide. Although it is not a big mountain, its isolation and its coastal position mean that

in clear weather it commands spectacular views, from Tanjung Datu at the westernmost tip of Sarawak to Gunung Santubong 90 kilometres (55 miles) to the east.

Staying at the Park

Accommodation has recently been completed at Gunung Gading and visitors can stay in either a hostel or chalets. The new interpretation centre is of interest not only for its exhibits and explanations about the park but also for its unusual architecture, based on the shape of the *Rafflesia* flower.

The park is hardly five minutes' drive from Lundu town, and if accommodation at the park is fully booked, the town itself can offer good alternatives. For those who have a little time to spare, Lundu is also a convenient base from which to visit the beaches of Pandan and Siar, to swim and relax. A visit to Gunung Gading can be incorporated within a trip to see Tanjung Datu or the limestone caves around the town of Bau. Another possibility would be to visit the Talang Satang Islands, which may become Sarawak's first marine park, protecting nesting turtles and other marine life.

Above, top: *The cabbage-sized bud of* Rafflesia tuan-mudae *appears.*
Above, centre: *The flower opens suddenly, revealing the smelly interior.*
Above, bottom: *Decay sets in after a few days, the flower melting away.*

BAKO NATIONAL PARK

Sarawak's First National Park

Bako was the first national park to be established in Sarawak, in 1957, and is still a showpiece in the system of protected areas. Covering about 27 square kilometres (10 square miles) of forest, it occupies a mainly sandstone peninsula on the South China Sea opposite Gunung Santubong. Its attraction is due partly to the wide variety of forest types within this small area, and partly to the impressive seascapes and rockscapes along the coast.

Characteristic Plants

Much of Bako National Park is on thin, white, sandy soils that lie over level sandstone plateaux at different levels above the sea. In places peat builds up, forming a thin, dark layer, with lots of tree roots but easily eroded or dislodged. This makes for an

Opposite, top: Seen from the beach at Bako, the legend-shrouded Gunung Santubong dominates the impressive view across the bay.

Opposite, bottom left: The monkey most likely to be seen at Bako is the Long-tailed Macaque, especially near the park headquarters where it searches for scraps of food.

Opposite, bottom right: The flying lemur or Colugo is nocturnal, glides from tree to tree rather than flies, and is well camouflaged when at rest.

Above, right: The squat pitchers of Nepenthes rafflesiana *growing near ground level are distinct from the slender ones higher up the same plant.*

environment very poor in nutrients. Characteristic of the forest are pitcher plants, ant plants and sundews. All such plants are able to acquire some nutrients from sources other than the soil. One of the most common pitcher plants at Bako is *Nepenthes ampullaria*, typically restricted to the ground. This is a species with fat round pitchers with slender lids. Insects perching on the slippery rim tend to fall into the soupy water inside, where they die and are digested. Sundews obtain nutrients from insects that settle on the leaves, which have sticky-tipped hairs and curl around any unfortunate victim.

The entire forest reflects the low nutrient status of the soils: rather stunted trees, especially on the exposed plateaux and where the sands form only a thin layer over the bedrock, with roots that penetrate little below the surface. It is easy to see the differences between forest growth in different parts of the park, along the coast, on the higher ground, and within the smaller valleys. Most distinctive is the patchy growth of mangroves in sheltered areas where sediment gathers. A good stand of mangroves awaits arriving visitors at Teluk Assam where the boats reach the jetty. The next bay south, Teluk Delima, also has some mangroves; here, these are mixed with clumps of the extremely spiny nibong palm.

Wildlife Experiences

It is usually difficult to find big animals in Sarawak's parks, because of former hunting pressures, but Bako is the exception. An impressive Bearded Pig or two can often be seen foraging in the forest close to the park

Map labels: Pulau Lakei; Teluk Limau; Tanjung Rhu; Teluk Keruing Trail; Sea Stack; Tajor Waterfall; Teluk Assam Park HQ; Tajor Trail; Lintang Trail; Teluk Limau Trail; Tanjung Po; Teluk Delima; Wildlife Observation Post; Bako National Park; Ulu Serait Trail; Paya Jelutong Trail; Bt. Gondol; Kg. Bako; To Kuching; Kuching; N

Location: About 40 km (25 miles) northeast of Kuching, the state capital, on a sandstone headland on the coast.

Climate: Hot by day, moderate temperatures by night. It is generally pleasant within the forest, but can be very hot in open sandy areas on the sandstone headland plateau.

When to Go: A good wildlife experience at any time of year; more migrant birds between September and March.

Access: Easily accessible by bus (or taxi) from Kuching to Kampung Bako, then by small boat to the park headquarters at Teluk Assam. Rough seas can prevent exit in afternoons, November–February.

Permits: Easily arranged at the office at Kampung Bako, where boats depart for the park. Accommodation must be booked in advance through the National Parks and Wildlife Office in Kuching.

Equipment: Light clothing and good walking shoes; swimming gear; sunblock cream. Insect repellent handy in the evenings.

Facilities: Information office, jetty, and simple chalets and hostel accommodation. Canteen, and trails through the park.

Watching Wildlife: Easier to see mammals here than in most other parks; Bearded Pigs and Long-tailed Macaques are usually to be seen around park headquarters. Do not feed the monkeys. Proboscis Monkeys occasionally give good sightings.

Visitor Activities: Walking, wildlife watching, plant observations. The sandstone formations along the coast offer good photography. Snorkelling around Pulau Lakei and Teluk Limau in the northeast of the park, about 8 km (5 miles) from headquarters.

headquarters, or behind the canteen. These tall, rangy-looking pigs are an important food source in Borneo. Both sexes sport great clumps of blond whiskers either side of the jaw. Their teeth are massive, much heavier than those of the Peninsular Malaysian wild boar, and are probably adapted to crushing tough, fibrous roots, tubers, and the hard seeds of forest fruits.

The visitor looking for Proboscis Monkeys may be lucky enough to find them anywhere in the taller forest, but they are most likely to be seen in one of the mangrove patches, perhaps at Teluk Delima, the next bay south from Teluk Assam. An encounter between groups, with two big males honking and displaying at each other, and their attendant females milling around, is impressive and exciting. These monkeys are among the few mammals that appear to be comfortable in the nibong palms, and can land with a thump upon a spine-riddled palm trunk, unharmed and oblivious to the formidable thorns.

About 150 species of birds have been found at Bako, a moderate total. It is one of the few places where a selection of waders, seabirds and forest birds can be found together. Between September and March there are usually a few Lesser Golden Plovers, Whimbrels or Curlew Sandpipers about. In the mangroves, look out for birds such as the Copper-throated Sunbird and the Mangrove Flycatcher. Seabirds occasionally pass by; a recent record was of a Red-footed Booby. Furthermore Bako, being on a peninsula, picks up a number of migrants such as Yellow Wagtails, Grey Wagtails, and a few rarities. The variety of birds is therefore better during the northern autumn and spring, when migration by waders and passerines is under way.

Exploration

Bako has a number of good, well-marked visitor trails (and maps at all junctions). One leads from the park headquarters south to Teluk Delima less than an hour away. The Lintang trail is a 5-kilometre (3-mile) loop through a variety of forest types, extending over the sandstone plateau but beginning and ending in better forest near the sea. It is also good to explore the coastline where, north of Teluk Assam in particular, wave action has sculpted the richly coloured rock into strange shapes.

For those interested in park management, Bako makes a good study. Visitor access is by boat, from the village of Kampung Bako across the bay, and is therefore highly controllable. Bako is extremely popular, with many tour parties arriving from Kuching, and is usually at its busiest from about June to August. To lessen impact on the environment, some trails are periodically closed for recovery of the ground and vegetation on the fragile white sands of the plateau areas.

Below: *Male fiddler crabs, with one big claw, have brilliant colours that differ from species to species.*

Above: *The accessibility of Bako National Park makes it an ideal location for local naturalists and school parties to visit.*

Left: *Near park headquarters, the tide inundates the breathing roots of mangrove trees.*

Opposite: *Richly coloured sandstone is characteristic of Bako's coastline.*

KUBAH NATIONAL PARK

A Crucial Site for Palms

For one group of plants, the palms, Kubah National Park is internationally recognized as one of the most important sites in the world. It had long been the intention of the authorities to create a national park in this area, a small and isolated hilly region west of Kuching and close to the village of Matang. This intention was achieved in 1989 and the park was named Kubah, a reference to the domed shape of its boundary. Gunung Serapi, on whose slopes the park lies, just falls short, at 911 metres (2,988 feet), of truly montane altitudes.

A Wealth of Palms

Ninety-eight species of palms have been recorded in just 22 square kilometres (8½ square miles) of hill forest at Kubah, making it perhaps the richest palm habitat for its size anywhere in the world. It is also historically important, palms having been collected here by the great Italian naturalist Odouaro Beccari in 1865, and several new palm species

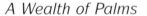

Opposite, top left: The rounded leaves of Licuala orbicularis *make it immediately recognizable.*

Opposite, centre left: A number of small streams and waterfalls are attractive features of the park.

Opposite, bottom left: Johannesteysmannia altifrons has bigger entire leaves than any other palm at Kubah, and is sometimes used for thatching.

Opposite, right: The foliage of stemless palms and rattans forms a graphic pattern in the forest.

Above right: The biggest Malaysian moth is the Atlas Moth, with translucent patches in its rich velvety wings.

were first described in this area. Eighteen species, virtually one-fifth of the total, are endemic to the park and its immediate vicinity.

Palms are a fascinating and unusual group of plants. Among the species found here are tree-like forms with tall, bare trunks; small, stemless palms of the forest understorey; and clambering rattans that cling and hoist their way up into the canopy. Visitors interested in visiting the nearest longhouse, at Rumah Jugah just outside the western boundary, can see many examples of palms being put to economic use, for matting, food, drink, weaving, basketry, furniture, house construction, and personal adornment.

Even the casual visitor to the forest is likely to appreciate the diversity and attractiveness of the palms themselves, for instance *Licuala orbicularis* with its decorative round-rimmed leaves; *Korthalsia flagellaris*, a species with fishtail-shaped leaflets and long thorny whips; and *Johannesteysmannia altifrons* with huge diamond-shaped leaves which give it the common name of Umbrella Palm. The more you look, the more you are likely to find in the way of unusual plants and subtle variations.

One reason for this richness in a single group of plants must be the relative isolation of these hills within the broad coastal plain of the lowlands. The hills are mainly composed of sandstone, and are therefore steep, and have some later intrusions of igneous and metamorphosed rocks here and there. The igneous rocks correspond with the main peaks, while the sandstone slopes are heavily dissected by streams and weathering that has, over millennia, added fine sedimentary material to the alluvial plains below.

Location: About 20 km (12 miles) west of Kuching, near the village of Matang, occupying slopes of Gunung Serapi.

Climate: Warm to hot by day, moderate temperatures by night. There may be rain at any time of year, but it tends to be wetter between about October and January.

When to Go: Any time of year.

Access: Quickly and easily accessible by car, or by bus from Kuching, taking about 1 hour; taxi may be a little expensive.

Permits: Can be arranged on the spot at the park headquarters; there is a small entry fee upon registration.

Equipment: No special equipment is necessary; light clothing and walking shoes or boots suitable for use in the forest. Bring binoculars for birdwatching, and a camera.

Facilities: Facilities for picnicking are available close to the entrance point. There are several trails into the forest. Recently completed accommodation. A wildlife centre is being established round the other side of park from the current headquarters.

Watching Wildlife: Birdwatching is possible along the trails, and along the road leading to the telecommunications station on Gunung Serapi. A variety of unusual palms and other interesting plants along the trails. Orchid display garden and insect breeding centre under development.

Visitor Activities: Picnicking, walking, birdwatching and photography are amongst the range of activities. Recreational centres are being developed outside the eastern boundary of the park. Longhouse to visit at Rumah Jugah.

Above: *The Yellow Birdwing butterfly seldom settles to allow a close view.*

Right: *The westward view from Gunung Serapi towards Kuching reveals the park's forested and rolling hills.*

Above: *Ease of access to Kubah National Park makes it a good destination for the amateur naturalist and day visitor.*

Animal Life

Kubah National Park is not the place to see big animals. Most of the gibbons and monkeys have gone. A few Bearded Pigs rummage amongst the undergrowth for roots, tubers and fallen fruits. Great Argus Pheasants were still fairly common until recently. Nevertheless, over 125 species of birds can be found in the park. All of these are lowland birds, because Gunung Serapi is not high enough to support a montane community. There are, however, some which prefer hill slopes, such as the Scaly-breasted Bulbul, Hill Blue Flycatcher and Blyth's Hawk-eagle. The Chestnut-crested Yuhina is one of these hill birds, perhaps the one species which could arguably be called montane, and endemic to Borneo.

An Important Refuge

The setting up of the park at Kubah has helped to contain pressures such as hunting and the collection of forest produce. Recreation is currently confined to the lower parts of the park, at the base of Gunung Serapi, and it seems unlikely that tourism pressures will spread significantly uphill. Kubah, in essence, provides a pleasant getaway where an informative look at the rain forest is possible for the general public.

BATANG AI
NATIONAL PARK

Conservation and Traditional Lifestyles

The Batang Ai National Park was created in 1991, and it is closely related to the impoundment of a huge lake that was formed by the building of the Batang Ai dam and hydro-electric complex. The lake lies outside the park boundaries, but it is an important part of the visitor's experience. There is also a resort here, designed so it has low impact on the environment, which employs a full-time naturalist. The eastern shore of the lake, away from the dam, gives access to the park along the upper reaches of the Sungai Engkari and Sungai Ai.

Wildlife Habitat

When Batang Ai was established, villagers had already been living in the vicinity for many generations. Park design, boundaries and management therefore had to consider the established usages, to minimize future conflicts and maximize opportunities for the residents to participate in development.

The result is a complex geographical situation in which undisturbed forest, cultivated land and traditionally used areas are interrelated. Batang Ai has one of the largest Orang-utan populations in Sarawak, and this was one of the prime reasons for its establishment. With impending extensions, the park borders the Lanjak-Entimau Wildlife Sanctuary and connects onwards to the Bentuang Karimun reserve in Kalimantan. These conservation areas cover 16,000 square kilometres (6,180 square miles) of crucial wildlife habitat. Batang Ai itself is 240 square kilometres (93 square miles).

It is very important for the park and its wildlife that visitors should approach it with clear and reasonable expectations. Orang-utans are difficult to see, but every visitor should be able to spot the nests they have made in the trees, and perhaps hear occasional calls. Sightings of the animals themselves are unlikely and should be regarded as a tremendous bonus, not a guaranteed experience. This point needs emphasizing, because complaints by visitors who demand that they see Orang-utans can place unnecessary pressures on the management authorities.

Hills and Rivers

The main rivers that flow southwest from the park into the lake are separated from one another by long hill ridges that rise from the water level to a maximum of just under 900 metres (3,000 feet). This means that the forest is all of mixed dipterocarp type, for the park does not reach montane altitudes. Climbing these ridges is hard work, but the ridge crests themselves tend to have forest with a rather open understorey. The highest points are where the park abuts Lanjak-Entimau to the northeast. This is extremely rugged country and does not provide a sensible route for getting from one protected area to the next.

Above the point where valleys have been flooded by the rising waters of the lake, the dipterocarp trees arch over the rivers. During the flowering season, their creamy

Above, right: An Iban elder in traditional dress. Older people adhere strongly to their cultural roots.

Location: About 180 km (112 miles) in a straight line east of Kuching, near Lubok Antu in Sri Aman Division.

Climate: Warm by day, moderate temperatures by night; usually quite comfortable within forest (and often cool at night) but can be hot in open areas around lake.

When to Go: Any time of year, but low water levels often in July–August may mean pushing boats upriver, and wet weather more likely in October–February.

Access: Overland from Kuching about 250 km (155 miles) via Serian and Engkilili, on roads of gradually declining quality, taking about 4 hours to reach Batang Ai dam. Boat from the dam to the park. Allow a full day for travel. Roads as far as main junction now very good, only the last 40 km (25 miles) unsurfaced.

Permits: Arrange with National Parks and Wildlife Office, Sarawak Forest Department, in Kuching.

Equipment: No special equipment is needed. Take clothing suitable for forest walking, including footwear with good grip (in case of pushing boats), leech socks, swimming gear.

Facilities: Accommodation in longhouses, usually arranged via tour companies in Kuching, or in hotel resort at lake outside park. Four trails through varied forest.

Watching Wildlife: Look for Orang-utans, gibbons, leaf-monkeys; occasional hornbills, various other birdlife.

Visitor Activities: Watching wildlife, forest walks and river travel. Local festivities.

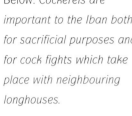

blossoms fall into the swift, clear water and are carried down to the lake margins. Rivers are a major means of travel and communication here, but during dry weather the water level in the rivers is low, and it is necessary to push boats upstream.

Because the park covers such steep land, visitors need to be fit for trekking. There is one relatively short trek to Bukit Sium and back, and another much longer trek up the ridge separating the two main rivers. This route then leads down to the bank of Sungai Lubang Baya, from where it is possible to take a boat back to the park headquarters.

The Longhouse Dwellers

The local residents are Iban people, longhouse dwellers who continue to practise a traditional way of life, partly dependent on forest produce and the harvests of their cultivated land. They manufacture a variety of handi-

crafts, such as the big rattan backpacks known as *selabit*, and decorative *Pua Kumbu* fabrics, woven in rich colours with symbolic patterns of birds, animals and mythical figures.

The communities formed a co-operative body in order to participate in tourism and help the Sarawak Forest Department in the conservation of the park. The Department has conducted several conservation education programmes and helped to arrange a business development training programme. With at least 350 local people having rights and privileges in the area, hiring them all to work in the park at any one time is impossible. At present some participate in an integrated conservation and development programme, working with tour operators or hotels, while others are employed by the park on a rotational basis.

One of the main attractions for visitors to Batang Ai is the chance to stay in a longhouse. This can normally be arranged by certain tour companies in Kuching which have established a relationship with the members of particular longhouses. Not all accommodation will be traditional – some separate 'tourist longhouses' have been built – but there may be opportunites to join in local festivities and participate in the community's social activities. The Iban are a hospitable people, but visitors should remember to be scrupulous in observing accepted etiquette and respecting privacy when necessary. Some of the profits from tourism remain within the longhouse communities, for schooling or for construction.

Success in endeavours to integrate the local communities into park management and tourism will help to protect not only the Orang-utan population, but also a variety of wildlife that includes six or seven kinds of hornbills, and Bornean Gibbons.

Lanjak-Entimau Wildlife Sanctuary

Immediately adjacent to Batang Ai, abutting the park's northern boundary, is Malaysia's largest wildlife sanctuary, Lanjak-Entimau. Here, in 1983, 1,688 square kilometres (652 square miles) of rugged hill forest around Bukit Lanjak and Bukit Entimau were set aside primarily for the protection of the Orang-utan. The sanctuary is closed to tourists, being intended solely for conservation and research. However, it merits coverage here as an important example of Malaysia's commitment to the preservation of wildlife.

Lanjak-Entimau, in fact, protects much more than Orang-utans. Survey work suggests that there are well over 200 bird species, maybe 150 reptiles and amphibians, and getting on for 100 mammals. In the early morning the sanctuary is filled with the haunting wails and resonant bubbling calls of Bornean Gibbons pronouncing ownership of their territories. They live in monogamous families of mother, father and offspring, each family with its own forest patch. Young adults must leave their parental home to find mates and establish their own domestic arrangements. Lanjak-Entimau also harbours many groups of monkeys, including the little-known White-fronted Leaf-monkey. This species has a startlingly brilliant white blaze in the middle of its forehead. It is found only in a very limited area of southern

Above, right: Rhinoceros Hornbills are still widespread and now totally protected; those in Borneo have a tighter curl to the horn than those found elsewhere.

Right: Bamboo has numerous practical uses. Here, rice, packed in lengths of bamboo, is cooked over an open fire.

Above, top: *Iban longhouses are typically built off the ground with access by somewhat rickety ladders.*

Above, centre: Pua *fabrics, woven by the Iban, come in both traditional and more modern designs and colours.*

Above, bottom: *Dancers' costumes often combine every-day clothes and ceremonial items, an indication of the often spontaneous nature of a performance.*

Right: *The lake at Batang Ai, access point for every visitor, presents a new context within which the area's wildlife, culture and tourism have settled into harmonious patterns.*

Above and below: *The protection of Batang Ai and adjacent Lanjak-Entimau allows Orang-utans to roam over a wide area of undisturbed forest.*

Sarawak and adjacent Kalimantan, and depends on Lanjak-Entimau for its long-term survival.

Sarawak's emblem the *kenyalang*, or Rhinoceros Hornbill, is one of seven hornbill species protected here. In addition, there are spectacular eagles amongst the larger birds, as well as the Great Argus Pheasant and the mysterious Bulwer's Pheasant, a shy bird found only in Borneo. This is one of its last refuges.

The Mixed Forests of Lanjak-Entimau

The sanctuary conserves one of the largest undisturbed blocks of forest in the southern part of Sarawak. Much of it is mixed dipterocarp forest, the remainder consisting mainly of heath forest, or *kerangas*, occurring on exposed ridges and hilltops. Just over the international border, Indonesia has created the Bentuang Karimun National Park and the result is a great sweep of transfrontier protection, making this one of the most important areas of conserved rain forest in the world. In fact, the area is so large that it has an impact on the local climate, the mossy forests acting as a condenser and collecting point in promoting rainfall.

These forests have a practical value for the local people as living space for the animals, such as the Bearded Pig, which they hunt for food. They also provide protection for the upper catchment areas of numerous rivers that radiate out from Sarawak's central high ground. The biggest of these is the Katibas, a fierce river that is only navigable into the sanctuary by those who are prepared to brave powerful rapids and drag their boats over boulders that are in places as large as houses. Heavy rainfall can turn a shallow stream into a mighty river overnight and camps must not be close to riverbanks.

Lanjak-Entimau: A Genetic Storehouse

Surveys have already identified more than 140 different types of medicinal plants in Lanjak-Entimau, plus a number of wild fruits and nearly 40 jungle vegetables that the local people use. The collection of seed material or small numbers of individual plants for research purposes is unlikely to damage the ecosystem and would amply justify the conservation of this forest as a genetic storehouse. Batang Ai and Lanjak-Entimau thus have differing and complementary purposes.

SIMILAJAU NATIONAL PARK

Coastal Forests and Sandy Shores

Along much of Sarawak's sandy coastline, exposed to all the force of the South China Sea, turtles come ashore to nest and their presence was one of the reasons for the creation of the Similajau National Park in 1976. The park is a narrow strip of coastal forest, about 3 kilometres (2 miles) wide but more than 25 kilometres (15 miles) long, within the much larger Similajau Forest Reserve. This neighbouring forest is very important, as it helps to provide a large enough area to maintain viable populations of some of the larger and more wide-ranging animals such as Bornean Gibbons and Rhinoceros Hornbills.

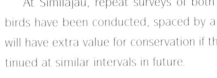

Marine and Forest Animals

Because it is next to the shore, Similajau has an interesting mix of sea-going and lowland forest animals. Amongst the larger sea creatures, Green Turtles are perhaps the most likely to be seen. The best chance of finding a nest is to walk along the beach early in the morning to look for the female's distinctive tank-like tracks leaving and re-entering the water. While on the beach it is also worth glancing seawards occasionally, just in case there are any porpoises or dolphins around. The Finless Porpoise is one species which comes fairly close inshore, and a rounded glistening back could be seen.

One of the beauties of Similajau is that, being in the extreme lowlands, it harbours many of the birds and mammals that are characteristic of really low lying forest. Important examples here are Storm's Stork, Black Wood Partridge, Wrinkled Hornbill and Bornean Bristlehead. The Bristlehead, never yet photographed, is of special scientific interest being related to the Australian butcherbirds.

There is a single main trail at Similajau, leading northeast from the park headquarters and ending at the coast. In the forest, anywhere along this trail, you may catch sight of the local black form of the Banded Langur or Leaf-monkey. This is an endangered primate, and Similajau offers the best chance of seeing it.

Flying foxes, the world's largest bats, are sometimes seen over the park at dusk, and can be common. The pattern of their movements and the reason for their more frequent appearance at some times of year are still poorly known. A study of this species, always at risk from hunters, is now being carried out in Sarawak for conservation purposes.

At Similajau, repeat surveys of both mammals and birds have been conducted, spaced by a decade. These will have extra value for conservation if they can be continued at similar intervals in future.

Swamp and Heath Forests

Part of Similajau's attraction is its patchwork of different forest types, one of which, now becoming rare, is freshwater swamp forest. This is found in a few flat, low-lying areas of the park, and has a peaty soil which is usually wet underfoot, with many swampy hollows. It can be hard going avoiding the wetter patches, and clambering over the stilt-like roots of the trees and the spiky leaved pandans. A very attractive and characteristic plant in this habitat is the Sealing-wax Palm, named for the brilliant orange-red leaf-bases that make it so easy to spot. It

Above, right: It is harder to see the Bornean Gibbon in the forest canopy than to locate its bubbling calls.

Location: A 26-km (16-mile) stretch of coastline, between Sungai Likau and Sungai Similajau, to the northeast of Bintulu.

Climate: Hot by day on the coast, more equable within forest shade, warm by night with sea breezes. Wetter weather with stronger winds and higher seas between about October and January.

When to Go: Any time of year, but generally milder weather March–September.

Access: From Bintulu by road to the nearest access point near Sungai Likau. Buses and taxis are the simplest ways to travel.

Permits: Registration at the park headquarters.

Equipment: No special equipment is required. Sunblock for beach. Swimming gear useful.

Facilities: A park office, headquarters and registration centre; limited accommodation. Forest trails, picnic and camping areas.

Watching Wildlife: Birdwatching provides a mixture of open country, scrub and forest birds, some rarities and endemics. Limited big mammals include Bearded Pigs and deer. The only national park in which to see Black Banded Leaf-monkeys. Occasional Green Turtle nestings occur on the beach. Flying foxes are common at some times of year.

Visitor Activities: Mainly weekend recreation such as picnicking, bathing, or taking short forest walks. More enterprising visitors can explore the different types of forest, and wander the shoreline for long distances.

Above: *Turtle Beach is one stretch of the extensive sandy coastline fronting the park along the South China Sea.*

Right: *Among several birds dependent on the lowland forest, and therefore vulnerable, is the Wrinkled Hornbill.*

thrives quite well in urban gardens and wild populations are coming under pressure as a source of plants for cultivation – fortunately, those at Similajau are protected.

In the patches of heath forest at Similajau, known also as *kerangas*, a different community can be found.

Here the soil is sandy, the canopy low, and most of the trees are pole-like and slender. Pitcher plants are particularly common in such sites, and the tub-shaped *Nepenthes ampullaria*, usually growing on or close to the ground, is the common species at Similajau. The bird community here is generally a poorer version of that found in tall inland forest, but there are some interesting specialists. One of these is the Hook-billed Bulbul, a species found only in Sumatra and Borneo, and apparently confined to forest on poor soils. Another is the pretty and increasingly rare White-throated Babbler, which looks reminiscent of a flycatcher with grey breast and white eyebrow and throat.

Beaches

It is always worth a walk along a sandy tropical shore like the one found at Similajau, for although there are

Left: Bauhinia, *a climber in the pea and bean family, is a widespread source of nectar for butterflies and other insects.*

Below: *Green Turtles nest annually along the beach, travelling long distances at sea in order to return to traditionally used sites.*

fewer creatures than in the mangroves, little can beat the pleasure of walking over the wet, wave-lapped sand and enjoying the view out across the South China Sea. Keep a look out for the ghost crabs, small pale-coloured crabs that skim along the beach faster than a man can run. The shore is also quite good for shells, especially cowries and cone shells, though most are small and worn down by the action of the waves and sand.

About midway along the park's shoreline is Golden Beach, named after the colour of its sand. From here it is possible to take a boat, by pre-arrangement with the park's staff, out along the coast and up the next river to the north. This leads to rapids and a bathing spot. Crocodiles have been reported from this area, and the risk is not to be taken lightly, but Sarawak's most famous man-eating crocodile episodes have all occurred far from Similajau.

NIAH NATIONAL PARK

Southeast Asia's Famous Caves

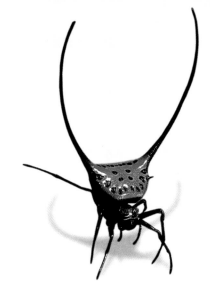

Niah is the premier archaeological site in Southeast Asia, gaining its fame in the 1950s when excavations in and around the limestone caves of the area revealed that humans had settled here 40,000 years ago. The national park that now protects Niah incorporates an arrowhead-shaped massif of limestone nearly 5 kilometres (3 miles) from end to end, together with the surrounding forest which is of interest itself for its wildlife.

The Great Cave

By far the biggest of the caves is the Great Cave, with a vast mouth, widening inside to a huge chasm in and out of which bats and swiftlets fly in their millions. This cave leads right through the limestone and has at least five main entrances, all out of sight of one another. On the long trek through the system from one entrance to another, walking is assisted by steps and sections of boardwalk. Up one slope and down another, round a corner, between giant boulders you

Opposite, top left: Skylights created by the roof's collapse provide dramatic lighting in parts of Niah's cave system.

Opposite, bottom left: The park's boardwalk is used by both visitors and the collectors of guano from the caves; guano is bagged and sold as a fertilizer.

Opposite, right: The Great Cave at Niah was once inhabited at its light-filled entrance.

Above, right: The Spiny-stomached Spider looks fearsome but its spines are harmless.

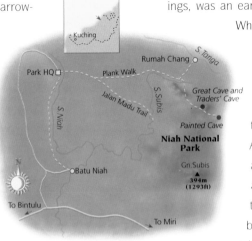

walk through the cave until there before you is the filter of light from one of the other openings.

The Painted Cave

This cave, remarkable for its prehistoric wall paintings, was an early Sarawakian burial chamber. When it was discovered, archaeologists found in a scattered line upon the floor, boat-shaped coffins, each with a strangely carved bowsprit, many of them fallen and broken open. All about lay remains of bones amongst seashells, earthenware and stoneware pottery. Access to the Painted Cave is restricted but you may be able to hire a guide by prior arrangement.

Cave Inhabitants

The current biological importance of Niah Caves is in the colony of mainly Black-nest Swiftlets, with some Mossy-nest and White-bellied Swiftlets. The nests of the former, used to make bird's-nest soup, have been collected here by traditional methods for centuries. The nest collectors could until recently be seen at work, climbing to the ceiling on long, precariously balanced poles. Bird and bat guano, used as fertilizer, is also collected extensively from the cave system.

Niah Caves contain the world's first ever (and perhaps only) earwig sanctuary, now subsumed within the park and cave system as a whole. This is a tiny portion of a cave floor, below a roost site of Naked Bats, a species which harbours an ectoparasitic earwig that feeds on the bat's flaking skin. Occasional earwigs fall off, landing with a plop on the ground below.

Location: 80 km (50 miles) south to southwest of Miri, in northeastern Sarawak, some way off the road from Miri to Bintulu.

Climate: Warm in the forest by day, can be a little cool at night; rain is frequent.

When to Go: At any time of year, but rain is likely to be heavier and more frequent throughout the November–January period.

Access: By bus or taxi from Miri or (slightly more distant) from Bintulu. The journey takes about 2–3 hours.

Permits: Should be obtained from the National Parks and Wildlife Office in Miri or Bintulu. Permits for entry to the Painted Cave may be discussed with the headquarters in Kuching, but access to this sensitive site is restricted.

Equipment: No special equipment is needed other than light clothing suitable for walking in the forest. Photography in the caves may require specialized flash equipment. Take a torch.

Facilities: Chalets and resthouses at the park headquarters; food and accommodation are available at Batu Niah village about 30 mins walk away. A museum has been constructed close to the park headquarters.

Watching Wildlife: Look out for swiftlets. Amongst other wildlife are Long-tailed Macaques, Water Monitor lizards, and a wide variety of birds. Flying foxes occasionally pass over at dusk.

Visitor Activities: Mainly bird-watching, swiftlet watching and bat watching. Caving (other than the usual entry to the caves on foot) and rock climbing are not allowed.

Right: *At the left of the vast mouth of Niah's Great Cave stand the research huts; the archaeological trenches are on the right.*

Opposite: *The dramatic colours of the lizard* Gonocephalus grandis *intensify when the male is alert and aggressive.*

Above: *Massive buttress roots provide support to giant forest trees through tension or pulling, rather than by acting as props.*

Right: *In the gloomy reaches of the caves the ground is caked with algae but few leafy plants can survive in the dim light.*

Out in the Forest

Outside the caves, besides swiftlets, it is sometimes possible to see the predatory Bat Hawk, as well as a variety of forest bird life. More birds are visible during the walk from the accommodation at base camp to the caves. Buffy Fish-owls can occasionally be seen along the stream. Over the Sungai Niah, besides Pacific and Barn Swallows, an isolated Striated Swallow may appear, quite a rarity. Around the chalets, Pink-necked Pigeons and various munias feed and nest in the densely foliaged fruit trees. Red-bearded Bee-eaters call hoarsely from the forest canopy, and sometimes nest in earth banks within the cave mouth.

Besides the walk to the Great Cave, parts of which are along a boardwalk, two less used trails are good for wildlife watching. The Jalan Madu trail passes through swampy forest near the river, while the Jalan Bukit Kasut trail leads from riverine forest up through heathy *keran-gas* forest to an altitude of 300 metres (1,000 feet).

Fossil Mammals

Most of the animal life that occurs in the park is the same as that which occurred there millennia ago, as many semi-fossilized examples show. However, these animal ancestors tended to be larger than their living relatives. The one fossil species at Niah which is totally extinct now is a Giant Pangolin.

Four other mammals that are extinct in this part of Borneo today have been found in the excavations. They are tiger, tapir, Javan Rhinoceros and elephant. Although their remains at Niah indicate that they were probably hunted by man during the Pleistocene period, it is thought that climatic change, not hunting, was the reason for their demise. Another two mammals, the Lesser Gymnure – an insectivore, resembling a large shrew in appearance – and the Ferret Badger, have each been identified by a single fossil example, and do not occur there today. In modern times they are montane, and again climatic change was probably responsible for their loss in the lowlands around Niah.

LAMBIR HILLS NATIONAL PARK

Botanical Riches in the Rain Forest

Lambir Hills National Park, established in 1973, protects a forest area of 70 square kilometres (27 square miles) on a small outcrop of rugged, scenic sandstone hills. It is the most diverse site in the world for trees. More than 900 diffferent species have been found in just one tiny area of only 0.5 square kilometre (⅕ square mile). Besides that, the steep and isolated peaks have provided a centre for the evolution of smaller plants which visitors can see along the more remote trails.

The park is fairly typical of the lowland mixed dipterocarp forest that occurs in northern Sarawak, except that it is much richer in species. The smaller plants include *Licuala* palms (known locally as *gernis*), which have been chosen as the symbol of the park because this group is both abundant and diverse here. The herbs include various aroids, gingers and terrestrial orchids, and there is said to be a higher proportion of rare and endemic plants here than anywhere else on earth.

Wildlife

In contrast to the rich flora in Lambir Hills, animal life is relatively scarce, but about 150 species of birds, 32 mammals, and many reptiles, amphibians and fishes occur. Overhunting of animals in the surrounding land

Opposite: Within 30 minutes' walk of the park headquarters are Latak Falls, the most scenic of the park's waterfalls and its most popular swimming spot.

Above, right: Basketwork, some of it in everyday use, is an extremely popular purchase with visitors.

has been a problem. It is not known how this will affect the plant community in the long term, owing to the scarcity of seed dispersers or pollinating animals.

The remaining wildlife includes Long-tailed Macaques, probably Malaysia's commonest monkey, and Pig-tailed Macaques. Birds, more conspicuous than the mammals, include the scarce Bornean Bristlehead. A Scarlet-rumped Trogon or a Dwarf Oriental Kingfisher may be seen in the forest understorey, and hornbills, including the Wreathed Hornbill, are present.

Waterfalls and Trails

One of the most attractive aspects of the park is the presence of many waterfalls. Three along the Sungai Latak are particularly popular with visitors and eight major falls occur at points on the southern slope of the main Lambir ridge. Along the Sungai Liam there are a further three; near the first two there are several shallow pools where children can play. The third and most distant fall from the park headquarters is 25 metres (80 feet) high and drops straight into a big pool suitable for swimming. Opposite the waterfall is a stretch of sand just right for picnics.

The twelve jungle trails in the park are well marked. Some link headquarters to the waterfalls and all give visitors the opportunity to view the interesting vegetation, animals, birds, insects and other features that the park contains. Walks can be as short as 15 minutes each way, or, for enthusiastic trekkers, as long as six hours for the trails that lead to the two viewing points at the top of Bukit Lambir and Bukit Pantu, 400 metres (1,300 feet) above sea level. In clear weather these look-outs give a

Location: About 32 km (20 miles) south of Miri in northeastern Sarawak, adjacent to the main Miri-Bintulu road.

Climate: Hot throughout the day although equable within the forest; warm by night. The weather is usually wetter during the period November– January.

When to Go: Any time of year is suitable for a visit.

Access: Accessible from the main Miri-Bintulu road which is serviced every day by bus and taxis. The drive takes about 30 mins from Miri.

Permits: Entry and camera fees payable at park HQ. Bookings for accommodation must be made through the National Parks and Wildlife Office in Miri.

Equipment: Light clothing and footwear suitable for walking in the forest; swimming gear.

Facilities: Reception/information centre, chalets and restaurant/shop. Temporary campsites beside the park headquarters equipped with basic amenities, lavatories, picnic tables. Shelters and barbecue facilities beside some of the waterfalls.

Watching Wildlife: Low altitude jungle primarily of botanical interest. Bornean Bristleheads can sometimes be seen in the canopy. Few large mammals occur, but monkeys and some small mammals may be seen.

Visitor Activities: Jungle walking, trekking and swimming as well as watching wildlife. Well-marked trails near the headquarters lead to many little waterfalls, and to the summit of Lambir Hills. Excellent birdwatching in all areas. Longhouses and an Iban handicraft centre near the park.

Above: *Trails at Lambir Hills have sturdy bridges, are well marked, and offer good views of the enclosing forest vegetation.*

Right: *The leaf of the fan-palm* Licuala valida, *like others in the genus, comprises a fan of leaflets divided to the base.*

fine view of the vast flat coastal plain of northern Sarawak, and both the town of Miri and the limestone outcrop of Niah Caves may be visible.

Studying the Rain Forest

Since 1965 Lambir Hills has become an important site for tropical rain forest research. Long-term ecological plots have been established to monitor tree growth rates, mortality, regeneration, forest structure and species composition. Stands of trees have also been established to study flowering and fruiting patterns. Lambir Hills is the only site in the world where long-term studies of climbers have been done in the rain forest. Further recent initiatives include a one-kilometre-long (½ mile) canopy walkway to facilitate research on pollination, and field stations for visiting researchers.

As the park is easily accessible from Miri, and other nearby towns and districts, it is popular with Malaysian visitors, especially at weekends, and offers excellent scope for nature education, for students and other interested groups. Conducted tours and special programmes can be arranged by the National Parks and Wildlife Office upon request. There is also a plan to establish a forest museum, to cater further for education and study.

Iban Villages

Within the vicinity of the park there are several Iban community longhouses, some of which are often visited by tourists. Most of them are situated along the Miri-Bintulu road. One, Rumah Nakat, has a handicrafts centre, where various items made from forest produce are sold. Rumah Aji, situated about 5 kilometres (3 miles) from the park, is the biggest of the community longhouses here. It houses no fewer than 100 families, and presents a good impression of the traditional Iban village way of life. Needless to say, it is a favourite place to visit when coming to the park.

Even if visitors have no time to visit a longhouse, it may still be possible to see local crafts, such as baskets, hats and knife sheaths, on sale by the roadside. Depending on the time of year, there may also be wild durian fruits, beans, or other edible forest produce. This use of wild products emphasizes how important the forest can be to locals. Conservation therefore needs to be integrated not only into park management but also into the attitudes and practices of nearby people. So far as plants are concerned, Lambir Hills offers great opportunities to do this. The park is likely to become of increasing significance to conservation research, as work proceeds on the dynamics of a plant community surrounded by agricultural land, and where animal pollinators and seed dispersers may be in short supply.

Top right: Bauhinia *is a legume and a climber, often seen in flower but little studied because it grows in such an inaccessible place high in the canopy.*

Centre right: *The communal longhouse verandah is a convenient place to dry fruits obtained from the forest, and nuts and peppercorns from the fields.*

Bottom right: *Among the more eagerly sought mammals by hunters, the Barking Deer or Muntjak is now very rare around Lambir Hills.*

LOAGAN BUNUT NATIONAL PARK

Rich Birdlife of a Natural Lake

Loagan Bunut is a natural lake lying between the Sungai Tinjar and Sungai Teru in northeastern Sarawak. Here, in 1991, over 100 square kilometres (38 square miles) of water and surrounding land were set aside as Sarawak's ninth national park. The lake itself covers 650 hectares (1,600 acres), while the remainder of the park is mainly seasonally flooded peat swamp forest.

Wetland Birds

The rarity of such lakes in Malaysia would alone make Loagan Bunut worth protecting. In addition, it is one of the few examples of an open, not forested, natural landscape; virtually all other open spots in this humid tropical region are man-made. This habitat is created by fluctuating water levels. During and after wet periods, the level of the lake rises and drowns all but the most resistant vegetation, and during dry weather the level falls again to reveal flat, swampy areas that grow over with lush but short ground cover.

Opposite, top left: Like cormorants, the Oriental Darter must spread its plumage to dry after a prolonged spell in the water, where it swims almost submerged.

Opposite, bottom left: A totem carved from a tree trunk marks the secondary burial site of a respected Berawan individual. The burial jar stands below.

Opposite, right: During breeding, which is known from few places in Borneo, the face and leg colours of the Great Egret intensify and the bill turns black.

Above, right: The Blue-eared Kingfisher can be found in peat swamp forest near the lake.

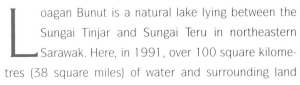

Within these swampy, grassed and reedy places live water birds such as herons, bitterns and egrets. Cinnamon Bitterns and Yellow Bitterns are small and rather colourful members of the heron family which can be seen foraging within this vegetation around the edges of the lake and, occasionally, in brief flight. Purple Herons probably nest within the areas of taller grass. The egrets such as Little, Intermediate and Great Egrets, all-white birds of extreme elegance, are so far known here only as migrants. So few records of nesting have been made for these species in Borneo that even casual birdwatchers can hope to add to the store of information, and there is every chance that at least some of these egrets breed in the vicinity of the lake.

These open wet habitats, for birdwatchers, provide a strange mixture of the exciting and the mundane. Some of the birds, such as Magpie Robins and Olive-winged Bulbuls, are as typical of town gardens as they are of remote national parks, and hardly arouse much interest. Yet others, particularly amongst the migrants, may be of special significance. The waders, shrikes, and the Grasshopper Warblers and other skulking passerines are groups that could produce important findings. The Oriental Darter, a member of the cormorant family, is one wetland bird that is internationally threatened, and for which the park provides protection.

Traditional Fishing

The shallowness of the lake, its dependence on seasonal rainfall, and the influence of developments outside the park make this a fragile environment. In dry weather, as the water recedes, the exposed mud forms a crust that

Location: About 80 km (50 miles) south to southeast of Miri, beyond Beluru, in the drainage of the Sungai Tinjar.

Climate: Hot by day, often extremely hot in open areas (can reach about 35°C/95°F), cooler along forest trails. Wetter weather tends to occur from about September–January.

When to Go: Any time of year; driest periods with shrinking water tend to occur in February and from May–June or July, depending on rainfall, adjacent river levels and with much variation year to year.

Access: Overland by the more inland road between Miri and Bintulu, via Beluru, reaching the edge of the lake area. Also possible to arrange river transport via the Sungai Baram and Sungai Tinjar, but this is usually slower and more expensive.

Permits: First contact National Parks and Wildlife Office in Miri, or in Bintulu.

Equipment: No special equipment is needed: light clothing, a hat to keep off the sun, sunglasses and sunblock lotion; strong footwear which will withstand getting soaked and muddied.

Facilities: Still under development; latest information should be sought from National Parks and Wildlife Office.

Watching Wildlife: Mainly birdwatching, on and especially round the margins of the lake, and in forest edge. Look out for darters, herons, occasional storks; hornbills and a variety of forest birds. Gibbons are audible most mornings.

Visitor Activities: Boating, forest walking, birdwatching and photography. Neither fishing nor swimming should be on your list.

cracks in geometric patterns, like paving slabs curled up at the edges, and becomes hard enough to walk on. Fish become trapped within the shrinking pools and not all can survive, many falling easy prey to birds. In particularly dry years a little puddle of stinking dead fish is not a rare finding here. The species are mainly catfish, a variety of smaller, less common freshwater natives, and nowadays a proportion of introduced tilapia.

Fishing is one of the cultural and economic bases for people living near the lake. The national park is therefore significant as an example of varied, effective, traditional fishing methods. Hand-held scoop or purse nets are interesting to see in use, but simple standing nets in deeper water are more common. Fish traps are made of rattan cane, bamboo and other plant products, and go by a number of local names according to their size, design and the type of fish they are patterned to catch. The method with the greatest cultural links is known as *selambau*,

which is a group effort to trap migrating fish shoals. These migrations depend on the water levels in Loagan Bunut and the nearby Sungai Tinjar, Sungai Baram and Sungai Bunut, and the fishing methods themselves are therefore seasonal.

Totems

There are still more interesting evidences of local culture. Those willing to arrange a journey across the lake and into the adjacent forest will be greeted with the sight of wooden standing totems. The significance of these in the religious beliefs of the people, and in relation to the areas of land worked by particular families, settlements or individuals, has some parallels with the well-known North American Indian totem pole. The concept of a standing carved tree trunk is similar, although the designs used and their meaning are quite different. Here, they are secondary burial places for hereditary aristocrats amongst the Berawan people.

Now that road access to Loagan Bunut has become possible, it is likely that the role of totems in the culture, and the role of the lake fisheries in the economy, will gradually alter. Protection of the lake and the adjoining forest within the park will help to ensure that any transition is managed smoothly and with minimum environmental change in this most unusual park.

Below: *Various groups of Kayan people live downstream from the lake towards the Tinjar and Baram rivers.*

Below, right: *Loagan Bunut is seasonal so water levels fluctuate. The brilliant green sedge-filled swamp is revealed during dry weather.*

A specially rewarding way of visiting Loagan Bunut, taking in as much of the traditional landscape as possible, is to combine it with a trip to Gunung Mulu National Park. With the help of a local travel company you can fly to Gunung Mulu, spend a few days there, then travel to Loagan Bunut by boat and return to Miri by road. This makes a trip with great contrasts.

Above, top: *Fish provide a major part of the diet for the Flat-headed Cat, a scarce nocturnal predator.*

Above: *Fishing traps made of bamboo and rattan are left standing in shallow water, and checked daily to obtain a sizeable and regular catch.*

Right: *The Purple Heron nests in small numbers in the sedges and reedbeds fringing the lake.*

Gunung Mulu National Park

Sarawak's Largest Park

The biggest and arguably the most spectacular of Sarawak's parks is Gunung Mulu National Park. Located in the northeast of the state, in Miri and Limbang Divisions, its 528 square kilometres (204 square miles) lie just south of the international border with Brunei Darussalam.

Steep, rugged limestone mountains and deep gorges run through the heart of the park. The Melinau Gorge and its river separate the peak of Gunung Api (1,750 metres/5,740 feet), with its astonishing limestone pinnacles, from that of Gunung Benarat before the river continues at a leisurely pace through the lowlands of the park. Further east, the more rounded sandstone peak of Gunung Mulu, first climbed in 1932, rises to 2,376 metres (7,796 feet).

The Caves

The outstanding limestone formations and caves have made Gunung Mulu internationally famous. Superlatives used to describe the caves include the biggest natural chamber in the world (the Sarawak Chamber, a vast unsupported dome); the largest cave passage known in the world (the Deer Cave); and the longest cave system in Southeast Asia (Clearwater Cave), in which over 100

Opposite: The Sungai Melinau provides an atmospheric approach to Gunung Mulu National Park from the visitor accommodation downstream.

Above, right: Long, narrow boats for the use of visitors regularly ply the park's river system.

kilometres (62 miles) of passages have been discovered and more may yet be found. These last two, and another two show caves known as Wind Cave and Lang's Cave, are open to visitors.

One sight that all visitors hope to witness is the tremendous display of bats emerging from the Deer Cave. This can be very variable depending on the weather, but on the best evenings more than a million bats emerge in successive waves taking more than an hour and a half. These are virtually all Wrinkle-lipped Bats, the other species in the cave leaving separately in small numbers. As the bats depart to feed over the surrounding forest, Bat Hawks and Peregrine Falcons take the chance to snatch a meal on the wing.

The Gunung Mulu Trail and the Pinnacles

The trek to Gunung Mulu's summit takes several days, starting with a long walk through lowland forest to the first camp at the base of the mountain. The climb then usually takes another two days up, ending at Camp 4 just below the summit. A further two days are needed to return all the way to park headquarters. In the summit zone, passing from lower montane forest into mossy ericaceous forest with rhododendrons and trees festooned with lichens, the trek occasionally involves scrambling up a wet moss-covered bank or holding onto tree roots, but is seldom seriously difficult.

The Pinnacles of Gunung Api are one of the park's most outstanding features. Created by the eroding

---

Location: In eastern Sarawak, about 100 km (60 miles) in a straight line southeast of Miri.

Climate: Hot by day, warm by night except in the forest, where it is more equable; cold nights when camping on the mountain. Rain can fall at any time of year; typically wetter between October and February.

When to Go: Any time of year, but during wet weather most visitor activities are more trying.

Access: Most visitors go from Miri either by air to Gunung Mulu (regular daily flights), or by river from Kuala Baram (the port outside Miri) to Marudi and Long Terawan, then boat to the park.

Permits: Should be arranged with the National Parks and Wildlife Office in Miri or Kuching. Tour companies will normally obtain permits for their clients; independent travellers should make arrangements (including booking accommodation) beforehand.

Equipment: Light clothes and strong, good-gripping shoes or boots for forest walking and for entering caves; strong torch useful. Specialist cavers should bring their own equipment.

Facilities: Park headquarters with information centre, chalets and canteen. Camping permitted at designated points (e.g. the summit trail). Boat services and guides. Boardwalk (to Deer Cave) and trail system. Four caves open to general public with lighting and walkways; specialist caving is available.

Watching Wildlife: Fine birdwatching everywhere in the park. Batwatching at Deer Cave (variable from day to day) with Bat Hawks, sometimes Peregrines.

Visitor Activities: Viewing caves, or specialist caving and climbing. Forest walks, trek to Gunung Mulu peak and limestone Pinnacles, with overnight stops. Birdwatching, photography.

Above: *A small community of Penan people lives close to the park. Here a Penan woman treads sago in the traditional way.*

action of water on limestone, these razor-edged stones protrude vertically from the stunted forest around their bases. Although limestone features of similar shape can be found in other parts of the country, none is so big as these; the Pinnacles reach over 60 metres (200 feet). Most are clustered on one limestone slope, and can best be seen either from the air or from the top point of the climb from Camp 5 (in the Melinau Gorge), which is about three hours walk.

As part of the park's management strategy, no trail maps are provided and all visitors must be accompanied by a recognized guide. Those going on the longer treks have to be accompanied by a park ranger.

Hornbills

It is difficult to find large animals in the park but hornbills can be seen and heard, especially on the treks to Camp 5 or to the summit of Gunung Mulu. A retching sound coming from the middle storey of the forest may reveal a pair of Black Hornbills, or a barking noise may herald the take-off of a small group of

Wreathed Hornbills from the forest canopy. Bushy-crested Hornbills live in extended family parties with several batches of grown young, and make a high-pitched yelping like a group of puppies.

Plant Life

The park's forests remain largely undisturbed and comprise a complex of mixed dipterocarp forest, peat swamp, forest over limestone, and montane forests. The plant life is of great importance. Along the 3-kilometre (2-mile) boardwalk leading to Deer Cave is a range of lowland forest, some of it growing on swampy, seasonally flooded ground. The rare *Cryptocoryne*, a little aquatic plant producing flowers like a miniature Arum Lily, grows in the everwet spots, while interesting limestone specialists grow closer to the caves. The climb to the Pinnacles is particularly rewarding to botanists. Pink-blossomed balsams, the flasks of pitcher plants, and an outstanding array of species of the One-leafed Plant group *Monophyllea* can be observed along the way.

The drama of Gunung Mulu: rugged limestone hills (above); bats emerging from the Deer Cave (right); Wind Cave rock formations (far right, above); the grandeur of Clearwater Cave (opposite, left); undisturbed plant life (far right, below).

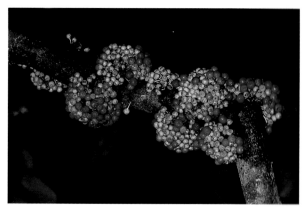

Local Communities

The local communities living around the park include Penan, Berawan, Lun Bawang and Iban people. The inhabitants of certain longhouses are allowed to continue to hunt pigs and deer, to fish, and to collect forest produce for food or handicrafts in specified areas of the park. Some of the Penan live in a permanent longhouse at Batu Bungan, immediately outside the park boundary. This has been incorporated into some tourists' itineraries on the way to or from Clearwater and Wind Caves. Remember to take off your muddy boots, before climbing the steps to look at some of the handicrafts such as baskets and bracelets.

Research at Gunung Mulu

Gunung Mulu National Park is being strongly promoted by the governmental and private sectors but many of its resources remain little known. Since the first big expedition by the Royal Geographical Society and the Sarawak State Government in 1977–78, international teams of scientists and explorers have visited the park but their expeditions have mostly concentrated on the caves.

Right: *The great height of the razor-sharp Pinnacles is revealed by the adjacent trees.*

Overleaf: *The Deer Cave is the biggest cave passage in the world, and is home to over a million bats.*

THE KELABIT HIGHLANDS

Heartland of a Mountain Community

The Kelabit Highlands lie in the mountainous centre of Borneo. Despite elevations of between 980 to 1,065 metres (3,200 – 3,500 feet) they are in fact an inter-montane basin ringed by even higher mountain ranges and peaks. On the western side, the Tamabu range isolates the basin from easy communication with the coast of Sarawak, while to the east the area of approximately 1,500 square kilometres (580 square miles) is flanked by the Apo Duat range which forms a natural border with Kalimantan. To the north sits majestic Gunung Murud, Sarawak's highest peak at 2,422 metres (7,946 feet). Those who have climbed this mountain are often spellbound by its magical mossy cloud forest. Lush montane forests and heath forests cover its slopes and

surroundings in a cloak of green that enhances nature's rugged beauty in one of the few places that remain virtually untouched by human activities.

The rivers of the Kelabit Highlands, the Pa' Dabpur and Pa' Kelapang, are fast-flowing rapids, strewn with boulders and quite unnavigable. However, some of them form the headwaters of the Baram and other rivers important for communications in the lowlands. The main means of travel in the highlands is to go by foot along forest trails.

Highland Forests

Much of the forest in the Kelabit Highlands, because it grows on heavily leached white sands, is either heath forest or dipterocarp forest that shows some characteristics of heath forest. At higher altitudes, where the cloud cover creates more prolonged and higher humidity, the forest is mossy. In the most heath-like areas, ant plants can be found, one or two of them the same species as found in Bako National Park. But because the forest here is at a higher altitude the tree community is quite different. There are gigantic *Agathis* trees, a Malaysian conifer with broad, not needle-like, leaves. Another conspicuous tree is *Casuarina nobilis*, which looks more like a typical conifer but in fact belongs to a different genus.

Mammals

Bearded Pigs are amongst the commonest big animals and are an important source of food for highland communities. There are also Sambar Deer (in Borneo known as *payau*) and Barking Deer. Bears occasionally come

Opposite, top left: *The range of the Binturong, the biggest of the civets, just reaches into montane forest here.*

Opposite, centre left: *The temperate climate of the highlands makes it possible to grow a range of vegetables.*

Opposite, bottom left: *The Malay Civet lives on a variety of small frogs, insects and other animals, which it catches mainly from the forest floor.*

Opposite, right: *Level plateaux between the mountain peaks enable wet rice cultivation to be carried out at the high altitudes of the Kelabit Highlands.*

Above, right: *Globba atrosanguinea is one of the smaller wild gingers found here.*

Location: The eastern edge of Sarawak, bordering Kalimantan (Indonesia), a montane basin south of Gunung Murud.

Climate: Temperate by day, 21°C (70°F), and cool to distinctly chilly at night, 14°C (57°F), with high rainfall.

When to Go: Any time of year is possible, but usually better outside the rainier period from October–February.

Access: By air; daily flights from Miri, Sarawak, via Marudi to Bario or twice a week to Long Lellang or Long Banga. Be prepared for delays and cancellations, as mist and rain may prevent landings in the highlands for several days.

Permits: Not required.

Equipment: Bring sturdy clothing and footwear for walking in wet, muddy conditions. Warm waterproof clothes and a sleeping bag needed for cold nights. Leech socks are useful.

Facilities: Longhouses are the main form of accommodation, but a few residents are now establishing guest houses. Do not abuse hospitality; a contribution to the household or possibly to the village may be appropriate. It may be possible to find a tour agency in Miri or in Kuching to facilitate trips to Bario and the Kelabit Highlands.

Watching Wildlife: Not much big wildlife, but plenty of good birdwatching and botanizing in cultivated areas and montane forest. The varied forest formations within a very short distance are a major attraction; each type has distinctive flora.

Visitor Activities: Walking and backpacking.

near the villages, especially during the fruit season when they can find windfalls on the ground in the orchards. One particularly interesting animal that has been seen here, and is known from scattered localities throughout Borneo, is the Tufted Ground Squirrel. This is one of the biggest squirrels in Southeast Asia, endemic to Borneo, and is a rich mahogany colour with long ear tufts.

The Kelabit People

This remote region is the heartland of the Kelabit people, Sarawak's only highland people and among the state's smallest ethnic groups, numbering fewer than 7,500. The main centre of the Kelabit community is the small settlement of Bario. In all, 19 longhouse settlements are

Above, left: Bearded Pigs are the Kelabits' single most important source of meat derived from the forest.

Left: The strange shape of Batu Lawi, a sandstone pinnacle, may account for its importance in Kelabit tradition.

Below: Long forest treks from village to village may involve crossing precarious bridges.

nestled throughout the highlands, some of the oldest established being at the villages of Long Dano, Ramudu and Pa' Dallih in the fertile Kelapang basin about one to two days' walk from Bario. Several other settlements are situated much further away. Long Lellang and Long Seridan occupy the upper reaches of the Sungai Tutoh and Sungai Akah respectively, while Long Banga and Long Peluan are found in the upper Baram. In this extensive area a potential national park, Pulong Tau, has been proposed by the Kelabit people themselves. This would encompass part of the Tamabu range as well as Gunung Murud and Batu Lawi, a spectacular monolithic sandstone outcrop which is of great significance to the local community. Pulong Tau contains the last few surviving Sumatran Rhinoceroses in Sarawak.

Rice Cultivation

One of the most astounding and enduring impressions for visitors flying into Bario is the view of wet rice paddies neatly sculpted into the landscape, suddenly seen as the aircraft emerges from the dense cloud cover draping the mountains. The preference for this form of

farming, developed quite independently from other people, distinguishes the Kelabits from most other groups in Sarawak. Dry, hill rice farming is also carried out, and between these two forms of cultivation 32 varieties of rice are planted. One variety has gained unequalled fame; this fragrant white rice is known locally as *pade adan*, but is widely sought after throughout Sarawak and other parts of Malaysia as Bario rice.

Rice is the focus of Kelabit life in the highlands. In the longhouses, the day begins before first light as *nuba' laya*, a soft rice made from *pade tuan*, is cooked on the hearth over the glowing wood fire. As household members warm themselves around it, conversation invariably turns towards planning the day's agricultural activities. Each year is punctuated by the different stages in the rice planting cycle, with the harvest coinciding with joyous Christmas and New Year celebrations.

For most Kelabits, ethnic identity is inextricably linked with the highlands. This place provides a link with their past, and bestows a sense of continuity: a dynamic force which empowers them to participate actively in the rapid change taking place in Sarawak today.

Left: *Dress, handicraft skills and artistic performance all foster a strong sense of community, whether among the Kelabits or the neighbouring Kenyah, shown here.*

Below: *Elaborate beadwork incorporates the stylized curling horn of the Rhinoceros Hornbill, even when the design is abstract rather than pictorial.*

SABAH

Covering 73,711 square kilometres (28,460 square miles) of land, Sabah is the second biggest state of Malaysia and occupies the northeastern corner of Borneo. The coastline, about 1,800 kilometres (1,118 miles) long, is highly indented and convoluted, with many capes, bays and mangrove areas.

The rivers flowing towards the northwest coast tend to be short, steep and fast-running. Those flowing to the east are much bigger and slower, winding in mature fashion across extensive lowlands. The Kinabatangan, for example, Sabah's longest river, has various oxbow lakes, a broad floodplain with seasonally flooded forest, freshwater dolphins, and important riverine habitat for big mammals. The Sungai Segama and Sungai Sugut have many similarities.

The predominantly hilly north and west of the state includes the Crocker Range which runs from the Sarawak border northeast to terminate in Gunung Kinabalu, at 4,095 metres (13,436 feet) by far the highest mountain in Borneo and unmatched between the eastern Himalayas and western Irian Jaya. The enormous altitudinal range represented by Gunung Kinabalu, its geographical isolation, and the array of other habitats in Sabah, make the state one of the nation's richest in biological diversity. High on any visitor's list of things to see are Proboscis Monkeys, Orang-utans, *Rafflesia* flowers, and the weirdly shaped pitcher plants of the taller mountains.

The places described in the following pages can give only a taste of Sabah's diversity. They include parks, marine parks, wildlife reserves and areas still in the process of acquiring legal protection. Each has its special function. Danum Valley, for example, is a premier research area. Sipadan and the Semporna islands have some of the best coral reefs in the world. Pulau Tiga is small but important for one species of sea snake. Together, the protected areas of Sabah are intended to form a network which ensures the survival in perpetuity of a representative selection of natural habitats and their constituent species.

ULU PADAS AND LONG PASIA

Rugged Ranges and Ancient Forests

The mountain village of Long Pasia in the remote Ulu Padas region of southwestern Sabah is named for the distinctive red river, stained by tannins washed by rain from fallen leaf litter in the forests, which runs through it. In the language of the local Lun Dayeh people, *Pa* is the short form for 'river', and *Sia* means 'red'. Here, the Pa' Sia and the Sungai Matang meet to form the headwaters of the mighty Sungai Padas, second in size only to the Kinabatangan in eastern Sabah, and important to many towns and settlements in the lowland areas. The clear waters of these rivers are appreciated by the Lun Dayeh for the delicious fish they supply.

Opposite, top left: *Asian Fairy-bluebirds with their enamelled blue plumage are among the most spectacular of the smaller forest birds.*

Opposite, centre left: *Only at night do Leopard Cats emerge to look for small prey.*

Opposite, bottom left: *Wary and alert, the Crested Fireback Pheasant can be glimpsed only briefly.*

Opposite, right: *Brilliant red barked* Tristaniopsis, *related to the Australian gums, are a feature of the heath forest.*

Above, right: *The Lun Dayeh people live in close relation with their forested surroundings; traditional attire includes snakeskin and treebark cloth, and a wild boar's incisor.*

Previous pages
Page 128: *Sabah is renowned for its beaches, including those of Pulau Sapi in Tunku Abdul Rahman Park.*
Page 129: *Sabah's corals are of international ranking.*

Protected Forests

The rugged ranges of Ulu Padas at 1,200–1,800 metres (4,000–6,000 feet) are covered by untouched heath and montane forests containing a diversity of interesting plants, especially at higher elevations. Because of the area's inaccessibility, the flora of Ulu Padas has always been something of a mystery. However, surveys begun in 1997 have started to uncover a trove of exciting discoveries, including several species of orchids and gingers that may be completely new to science. *Eria aurantia* is a recently described orchid found in the heath forest, with leafy stems that grow to nearly twice the height of a man. Many other and more colourful plants occur.

In areas of old forest, impressive *Agathis* trees can be found, some so huge that as many as ten people would have to join hands to reach around them. Ensuring that these forests continue to flourish is important to the Lun Dayeh people, many of whom, particularly the older generation, have long appreciated the value of forest plants for their structural, material, edible and medicinal uses. The 'People and Plants' project between WWF Malaysia and the villagers aims to establish a permanent record of the traditional knowledge.

While there are two Virgin Jungle Reserves in Ulu Padas, most of this area is Commercial Forest Reserve which permits selective logging activities. Nevertheless, studies have been undertaken by the state government to support the establishment of further protected areas here, to ensure that this rare and exciting place continues to retain its rich natural wealth.

Location: An area of about 90 km² (35 sq miles) in the extreme southwestern corner of Sabah, adjacent to the borders with Sarawak and Kalimantan.

Climate: Warm by day, cool at night, especially in the forest and at higher altitudes, with fairly high rainfall. July and August tend to be drier months.

When to Go: At any time of year, but local residents are usually busiest with sowing or harvesting food crops in August/September and January/February. Least busy period is March–May.

Access: Malaysia Airlines flight by Twin Otter. This flies once a week from Kota Kinabalu to Long Pasia. Overland tracks require a 4-wheel drive vehicle, and may sometimes be impassable.

Permits: Not required for entry to the area. However, Immigration Department permission required for overland trek into Sarawak.

Equipment: Much scope for walking and trekking, so good shoes or boots, and strong comfortable backpack may be useful. Otherwise, light outdoor clothing, a sweater for cool evenings, and photographic equipment.

Facilities: No hotels; visitors must be prepared for homestay, either arranged on the spot or with a tour agency in Kota Kinabalu. Remember that you are guests of the village. Suitable for small groups, not large tour parties.

Watching Wildlife: Though not specifically a wildlife destination, good for birdwatching in open country, forest and forest edge.

Visitor Activities: Photography, walking, birdwatching, botanizing and river trips; many cultural experiences possible when visiting monuments and places of interest around the settlements.

Above: *Funerary dragon jars not only mark a burial and commemorate an individual, but also link the family members to a specific area of land.*

Right: *Fruits collected from the forest edge supplement and diversify the diet from cultivated crops.*

Below: *A sense of identity is strengthened by cultural performances specific to the Lun Dayeh community.*

A Cultural Heritage

To the Lun Dayeh, the land and the way they have used it through the centuries represents their heritage. They are skilled farmers, planting mainly dry hill rice and a variety of other food crops. Although, from the air, one gets the impression that Long Pasia is completely surrounded by forest, many of the areas are, in fact, former fields now lying fallow to allow the soils time to recover. These secondary forests will eventually be cleared again. Primary forest is rarely opened up.

Distinctive historical and cultural markers can be found throughout the forests surrounding Long Pasia, including impressive stone monuments, massive carved rocks and unusual crocodile-shaped mounds. Some are the tombs of important people laid to rest in *tajaus* or dragon jars, while many others are associated with Upai Semaring, a legendary being who left traces of his presence throughout the area – from enormous footprints on rocks to the ornate patterns, thought to be finger drawings, left on massive riverside boulders.

A Special Retreat

Long Pasia captivates visitors from around the world. Now a strongly Christian community, it is for many a special spiritual retreat and a place to commune with nature. Others are attracted by the adventure of hiking across the border to Sarawak on footpaths established by decades of use. The peaceful way of life in Long Pasia, its magnificent surroundings and the mysteries of its past hold something for all who go there.

PULAU TIGA PARK

Reef and Island Life

Pulau Tiga Park is a group of three islands. One, Pulau Kalampunian Besar, has been reduced by waves to a mere sandbar upon which Great Crested Terns roost at high tide, while another Pulau Kalampunian Damit, is a small rocky stub about 40 metres (130 feet) long and 30 metres (100 feet) high.

Pulau Tiga itself is 607 hectares (1,500 acres), a low, oblong island formed not from underlying rock but from ages of accumulation from the eruptions of mud volcanoes. These strange phenomena, sometimes no more than a metre (3 feet) across, are points where hot mud bubbles to the earth's surface at long and irregular intervals. At Pulau Tiga the rate of accumulation of dried mud has been fast enough to create a substantial island that resists the waves. Several active mud volcanoes can still be seen at the summit of the island. Pulau Kalampunian Besar was formed in the same way, but never attained the same size and was washed away.

The Park on Land

The park was created in 1978, and covers 158 square kilometres (61 square miles), most of which is sea. The vegetation of Pulau Tiga includes a mixture of relatively undisturbed forest and introduced trees. Strangling figs are abundant, producing fruits that are fed on by various pigeons such as Pied Imperial and Green Imperial. Towards the beach are some native trees like *Barringtonia*, which drop their magnificent, fluffy, pink and white night-flowering blossoms onto the sand each morning, as well as casuarina and coconut palms.

In the sand, often between the roots of a *Barringtonia*, the large, ground-dwelling birds known as megapodes will deposit their eggs. The species here, often called the Philippine or Tabon Scrubfowl, is a chicken-like greyish-brown bird with a bare red face and enormous feet which it uses to dig nesting holes and pile mounds of loose warm sand over its eggs. A succession of eggs is laid at intervals over a few days. They are deposited in a rather vaguely defined area and incubated by the temperature of the sun-warmed sand. Each egg – if it is not taken by a rat or monitor lizard – will hatch after a rather long interval, and the chick must then burrow up to the surface where it will fend for itself completely free from any attentions by its parents.

Other animals that can be found on Pulau Tiga include a few Bearded Pigs, and a few species of lizards and frogs. However, the park is much more famous for its sea snakes. On Pulau Kalampunian Damit and in the nearby waters there is a population of up to 800 Yellow-lipped Sea-kraits, pearly-blue coloured snakes ringed with black. Unlike most other sea snakes, this species spends a good deal of its time on land, and reproduces there. During the day, the snakes are quite inactive and docile, avoiding too much heat by hiding among boulders and under logs. At night, when they are at their most active, congregations of several females and many males can be found.

Above, right: *The Emperor Angelfish is one of the most strikingly coloured of Sabah's fish.*

Location: Marine area off the western coast of Sabah, 50 km (30 miles) southwest of Kota Kinabalu.

Climate: Usually hot and sunny by day, warm by night; there is more likelihood of rain from September–February, accompanied by rougher seas.

When to Go: Any time of year, perhaps best from March–June.

Access: Either by arrangement with boat owners at Kota Kinabalu, or by travelling overland via Papar to Kuala Penyu and arranging a boat from there.

Permits: Arrangements for a visit should be made with Sabah Parks office in Kota Kinabalu; accommodation must always be booked in advance. Special permission must be sought to visit Pulau Kalampunian Damit.

Equipment: Light clothing providing protection from the sun; swimming gear; scuba divers and snorkellers need to bring own equipment, or arrange with tour company; strong footwear if visiting Pulau Kalampunian Damit.

Facilities: Park headquarters with rest house, jetty and picnic shelters; there is a research station on Pulau Tiga.

Watching Wildlife: Megapodes, Great Crested Terns, various frugivorous pigeons amongst the birdlife. Yellow-lipped Sea-kraits are an amphibious sea snake abundant on Pulau Kalampunian Damit and in nearby waters.

Visitor Activities: Walking along trails, picnicking, swimming and snorkelling, birdwatching; mud volcanoes in centre of Pulau Tiga. Dive sites off the main jetty and mangroves nearby; southwest and southeast coral reefs larger and less visited.

Map labels: Kota Kinabalu · SOUTH CHINA SEA · **Pulau Tiga Park** · Pulau Kalampunian Damit · Pulau Kalampunian Besar · To Kota Kinabalu · Pagong-pagong Beach · Larai-larai Park HQ · *Pulau Tiga* · N · Teluk Kimanis · Kuala Penyu

Right: *Greens, blues and yellows are of almost fluorescent quality in many species of reef fish.*

The park headquarters are on the southwestern side of Pulau Tiga, from where there are several walking trails. It takes about 20 minutes to walk to the nearest mud volcano, which is situated in the centre of the island about 100 metres (330 feet) above sea level. There are also trails to Pagong-pagong Beach in the north and Larai-larai in the west of the island, both of which take a little over an hour to reach.

Snorkelling on the Reefs

On the reefs around the islands there is a range of soft and hard corals, crinoids and reef fish. One fairly accessible reef lies directly off Pagong-pagong Beach and there is a much bigger expanse of coral around the western and southern sides of Pulau Tiga. For a wider variety of snorkelling opportunities, visitors can use the sandbar of Pulau Kalampunian Besar as a base from which to explore the various coral outcrops in the centre and northern part of the park. Butterflyfish, clownfish and parrotfish occur here, and in crevices in the corals and rocks there may be moray eels, which are sometimes eaten by the sea snakes.

The most easily accessible reef, Beach Reef, is close to the jetty. Large stretches are exposed at low spring tides, and the back reef lies only a few metres from the beach. Deep water separates it from the central reefs,

Below: *The main beach at Pulau Tiga receives very little pressure from visitors.*

further west, which extend from 250 to 550 metres (800 to 1,800 feet) offshore.

The two biggest reefs lie off the southwest and the southeast corners of Pulau Tiga. Together they cover more than 85 hectares (210 acres) but they are not so easy to reach as the smaller reefs off the jetty. They offer a wide range of fish life and corals for the diver and snorkeller. Sea urchins and sea cucumbers are abundant, and easily seen because of their size. Most of these reefs are in good condition, with little human damage, and offer a variety of habitats not only for corals but for the associated animals and algae. Because dive companies are not established within the park itself, diving equipment must be brought in either by the individual visitor or by arrangement with a dive operator in Kota Kinabalu. It is worth it, for the whip corals and gorgonians alone.

Above: Linckia laevigata *is one of the bigger starfish, more than 30cm (a foot) across.*

Right: *A sweetlips comes to a cleaner station, where smaller fishes may pick off flaking scales or parasites.*

CROCKER RANGE NATIONAL PARK

Sabah's Largest Protected Area

The Crocker Range is a forest-covered mountain range which stretches in a southwesterly direction from Gunung Kinabalu towards the Sabah-Sarawak border. Visible from Sabah's west coast plains, though frequently shrouded in rainclouds, the peaks of the range are about 30 kilometres (19 miles) from the coastline and rise to between 1,200 and 1,800 metres (4,000–6,000 feet) above the sea and coastal plains.

The higher zones of the Crocker Range, previously gazetted as a forest reserve, became a national park in 1984. At 1,399 square kilometres (540 square miles), this park is the largest totally protected area in the whole of Sabah.

Forest Zones

The natural vegetation of the lower parts of the Crocker Range is hill dipterocarp forest, containing five species of rare dipterocarp trees confined to the foothills of northwestern Borneo. The forests of the upper zones are rich in oaks, chestnuts and conifers, and the fallen, hard fruits and cones of these trees litter the ground to provide food for various species of squirrels, forest rats and porcupines. The highest ridges of the range, often enveloped in mist, bear thick mossy forest containing orchids, rhododendrons and pitcher plants.

Opposite: With many wild and rugged areas this is perhaps the least explored of Sabah's parks.

Above, right: Hidden within the park is the strikingly marked Rafflesia pricei.

One of the botanical features of the Crocker Range is the presence of *Rafflesia pricei*, which occurs most commonly in the zone where dipterocarp forest starts to give way to oak-chestnut forest. The flowers, which are typically about 30 centimetres (12 inches) wide when open and relatively small for the genus, may appear at any time of the year. For most of the time, only the slowly maturing buds are visible. An interesting introduction to this unusual plant is provided by the Rafflesia Virgin Jungle Reserve, reached via the Kota Kinabalu–Tambunan Road, which protects one of the most accessible *Rafflesia* sites in Malaysia. Flowers are often but not always in view.

Elusive Animals

Bird life is diverse in the Crocker Range but all species are rather scarce. The sudden arrival of mist, cloud or rain, at any time of the day, reduces animal activity, and the forest becomes eerily quiet. However, during brighter spells, the constant rolling 'took-took-terrroook' call of the Golden-naped Barbet is a characteristic sound. There are few large animals, though the park boasts a small population of Orang-utans, which are very rarely seen. Other rarities are the Ferret Badger and the Hose's Civet, both elusive mammals which are confined to the mountain ranges of northwestern Borneo. The mammals most likely to be seen while walking in the Crocker Range forests are some of the mountain squirrels and the Mountain Tree Shrew, a dark brown squirrel-like animal with a pointed snout. Bears and various primates occur on the hill slopes.

Location: A long range of mountains forming the backbone of western Sabah, running southwest almost to the Sarawak border. Highest peak Gunung Alab, 1,964 m (6,442 ft).

Climate: Pleasantly warm by day, can be chilly at night. Sudden mist, cloud or rain at any time of day; wetter weather mainly October– February.

When to Go: Any time of year, the best months most likely to be March and September.

Access: By road, 2 hours from Kota Kinabalu via Tambunan to Keningau. Alternatively by road or rail to Beaufort, then by rail to Tenom. A circuit route is possible. Rugged terrain limits accessibility of areas within park.

Permits: Make arrangements with the Sabah Parks office in Kota Kinabalu.

Equipment: Clothing suitable for walking in forest, strong boots or walking shoes, poncho; some warm clothing for evenings.

Facilities: No public facilities within the park. Accommodation in the main towns surrounding Crocker Range (apart from Kota Kinabalu, these are Keningau, Tenom and Beaufort) and on the Crocker Range ridge, outside the park, along the Kota Kinabalu – Tambunan Road.

Watching Wildlife: Birdwatching, anywhere in forest and cultivated areas. Interesting plant life.

Visitor Activities: Some tour operators offer forest hiking trips in the northern part of the range, between Kota Kinabalu, Papar and Tambunan. Whitewater rafting on Sungai Padas has been permitted from time to time, but status should be checked before you visit. The various small towns and markets around the park perimeter are of great interest.

Above: *The mountains of the Crocker Range are, in some areas, fringed by terraced rice fields.*

Right: *Trekkers need to be well-equipped for hiking in this area; terrain can be tough and daily distances covered may be long.*

Below: *Men of the Murut ethnic group welcome visitors to their village.*

Travelling around the Range

There are several distinctive areas of interest within and around the range. The southern end is bisected from east to west by the Padas Gorge, through which swirls the mighty Sungai Padas. Long ago, a railway line was constructed along the gorge and this is still in service, providing the only practical transportation link between the towns of Tenom and Beaufort, as well as an unusual opportunity for visitors to view the rugged scenery of interior Sabah.

There are two roads crossing west to east over the Crocker Range, from Kota Kinabalu to Tambunan, and from Kimanis to Keningau. The former is surfaced and suitable for ordinary motor vehicles, but the latter, built in the 1970s to extract timber from Sabah's interior, is gravelled and a four-wheel drive vehicle is recommended, especially during rainy periods.

The Tambunan valley, situated at an elevation of about 800 metres (2,600 feet) immediately to the east of Crocker Range, is one of the most attractive areas

within a two-hour drive of Kota Kinabalu. Apart from irrigated rice fields, bamboos represent a special feature of Tambunan's scenery, being used locally in the construction of houses, fences, footbridges, irrigation pipes and baskets, in fact for every necessity.

At Lagud Seberang, in the fertile Tenom valley below the southeastern end of the park, the Sabah Agriculture Department is developing an agricultural park based on a well-established research station. Amongst its attractions are a 'living museum' of useful cultivated and wild plants, unusual tropical fruit trees, and native orchids and other plants with horticultural potential. Tenom is accessible from Kota Kinabalu by road, via Keningau, and by taking a railway train along the Padas Gorge, once famous for its whitewater rafting.

The Crocker Range National Park is perhaps the least known, and one of the least visited of Sabah's parks. Its importance is obvious as there is great potential for pioneering new routes and itineraries, as well as for conservation initiatives for both plants and animals.

Above: Visitors can hike along established trails with traditional rope bridges and log ladders or experience the thrills of the Padas Gorge at the park's southern end.

TUNKU ABDUL RAHMAN PARK

Five Historic Islands

Tunku Abdul Rahman Park, or TAR Park for short, includes five islands within a short boat ride from Kota Kinabalu. Together with the surrounding sea these comprise a protected area of nearly 50 square kilometres (20 square miles), of which two-thirds is water. The names of the islands are symbolic of their history and early discoverers. They are Pulau Gaya ('big'), Manukan ('fish'), Mamutik ('for shell collection'), Sapi (the sound of a lowing buffalo), and Sulug (commemorating the ancestry of the Suluk peoples of Sabah).

The Park's History

These islands have a surprising connection with the Crocker Range National Park, being part of the same geological formation, cut off towards the end of the Ice Ages when a rise in sea level occurred. Exposed sandstone outcrops still feature along the coasts of most of the islands, forming cliffs, caves, honeycombs and deep crevasses. Wave action accounts for these.

Of the early exploration of the islands, very little trace remains today. Pulau Gaya has a record of land acquisition by the North Borneo Chartered Company in 1881, followed by pirate raids in the late 1890s. Subsequently, only a Bajau village fishing community was left. This is still the site of a now thriving community. Pulau Manukan was the site of a stone quarry, and

Opposite: *Idyllic Pulau Sapi is only a 20-minute boat trip away from Sabah's capital city.*

Above, right: Nembrotha nigerrina *is one of the most conspicuously marked sea slugs, yet can be difficult to locate.*

the remains of the manager's house as well as some old graves can still be seen on the island.

TAR Park was established in 1974, to protect the unique island vegetation and fauna as well as the marine ecosystem, and to provide enjoyment for visitors. The area first gazetted included most of Pulau Gaya except for the Bajau village, and the whole of Pulau Sapi. In 1979 the area was increased to include Pulau Manukan, Pulau Mamutik and Pulau Sulug as well.

Shoreline and Inland Trees

The diversity of plant life on the islands is of great interest. From shoreline to the inner areas the vegetation changes, influenced not just by distance from the sea but by the substrate and by early land use.

The original forest now remains only on Pulau Gaya – a sanctuary for the only undisturbed coastal dipterocarp forest left on Sabah's western coast. *Dipterocarpus grandiflorus* is a huge tree which, unusually, forms pure stands on the southern side of Pulau Gaya. Its distinctive two-winged fruits, up to 20 cm (8 inches) long, can often be found lying along the trails.

Casuarina trees are found along the shoreline of all the islands, somewhat resembling Christmas trees though they are neither pines nor at all related to northern conifers. Further back from the shore the stilt-rooted coastal pandan grows. It has big round fruits and long stiff leaves from which straw hats and mats are woven. On more exposed parts of the coastline the ancient, palm-like cycad can be found. This is a living fossil representative of a forest type existing more than 150 million years ago, before the flowering plants evolved. The biggest ones are over 5 metres (16 feet) high.

Location: Island group 3 km (2 miles) offshore from Kota Kinabalu, capital city of Sabah.

Climate: Usually hot and sunny, with wetter weather and rougher sea crossings October – February.

When to Go: Any time of year is possible, though better to avoid wet season.

Access: 20 min by boat, from the waterfront at Kota Kinabalu.

Permits: Book accommodation with Sabah Parks office in Kota Kinabalu; report and register arrival at visitor centre on Pulau Manukan.

Equipment: Light clothing and walking shoes; snorkelling or diving gear.

Facilities: On Pulau Manukan are park headquarters with chalets, restaurant, recreational facilities, visitor centre and jetty, and a trail system. On Pulau Sulug are changing rooms, public lavatories, picnic shelters and tables. The other three islands have intermediate facilities, with overnight accommodation available on Pulau Mamutik, and camping possible (with prior permission of Warden) on Pulau Sapi.

Watching Wildlife: Mainly snorkelling and diving to watch fish and other reef life; White-bellied Sea-eagles and other birdwatching.

Visitor Activities: Picnicking, snorkelling, diving and nature watching; windsurfing, sailing and relaxing on beaches. Fishing (hook and line only). Pulau Gaya has Police Beach (Bulijong Beach) and Camp Bay as popular swimming, sporting and relaxing areas, good reefs, and forest trails. Pulau Mamutik and Pulau Sulug mainly for picnicking and swimming; Pulau Sapi for snorkelling and diving as well.

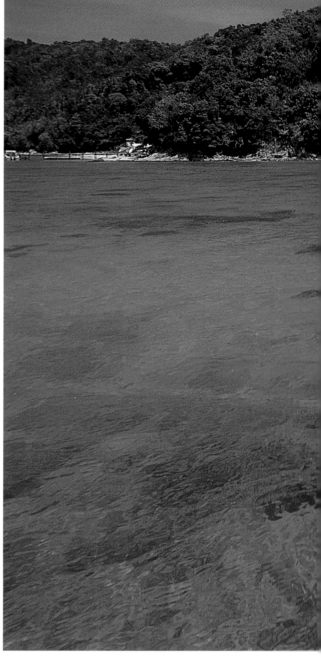

Away from the shoreline and the influence of the salt spray, you will find that the original forest, cleared long ago, has been replaced by secondary growth, inter-spersed with plants brought by man. These include coconut palms and fruit trees such as mangos, jackfruits and *terap* (a delicious relative of the breadfruit). Common ornamental trees include the coral tree and gardenia, whilst in the shaded gullies are palms such as the fishtail palm and the fiercely spiny nibong palm.

Nature Watching

Many birds dwell on the islands. White-bellied Sea-eagles can be seen flying over the sea, nesting on some tall isolated tree, or giving a display of aerial prowess, especially towards sunset. Pied Hornbills often fly over. Along the shore are Little Herons and various sand-pipers, and in the fringing vegetation White-breasted Wood-swallows, Pink-necked Pigeons, bulbuls, babblers, flycatchers and sunbirds. The curious, chicken-like megapode occurs here too, though it is rarely seen. The islands are an important transit point for migrating birds such as waders because, although the habitat is limited, this is the first land they may encounter after crossing the South China Sea.

Mammals on the islands include rats, squirrels and monkeys. Wild pigs are seldom visible, but signs of their presence include footprints and diggings where they have grubbed for roots. Occasionally, the Pangolin or Scaly Anteater can be found.

Marine Life

The fringing coral reefs are one of the main reasons why TAR Park was created, and they form an important part of the island ecosystem. Those around Pulau Manukan, Pulau Mamutik and Pulau Sulug are particularly attrac-

Below: *Anthias and other small fish can occur in massive congregations over the more complex-structured reefs.*

tive for visitors and excellent patches can also be found between Pulau Sapi and Pulau Gaya. In the ever-warm waters, corals, anemones, sponges, fan worms, sea cucumbers and feather stars all contribute to the diversity and colour. Easy access and good reefs now make this area a must for divers. All the smaller reef fish are present, and sightings of Whale Sharks are regular in the early months of the year.

Above: *Pulau Manukan offers superb snorkelling opportunities from the beach or direct from a boat.*

Right: *Different kinds of sea squirts cling to an unsteady substrate of pink and orange sponges.*

KINABALU PARK

Southeast Asia's Highest Mountain

Kinabalu Park was established in 1964, and protects 754 square kilometres (291 square miles) of extremely diverse country, from lowland forest up to bare granite peaks. The park's outstanding feature is Gunung Kinabalu, the highest mountain in Southeast Asia, reaching 4,095 metres (13,436 feet) at Low's Peak, one of several peaks of similar altitude in the summit zone.

Gunung Kinabalu is still rising imperceptibly, and broods over the landscape of Sabah; in clear weather it is visible from an enormous area of the state. At about 3,900 metres (12,800 feet) a rocky crescent, with two arms known as the western and eastern plateaux, embraces Low's Gully, a precipitous-sided black hole that is over a kilometre (nearly a mile) deep in some places.

Opposite, top left: *The shiny, deep purple orchid* Bulbophyllum vinaceum *seldom has more than a single waxy blossom on any one plant.*

Opposite, centre left: *Birdwatchers along the trails are likely to see montane specialists such as the Indigo Flycatcher.*

Opposite, bottom left: *Kinabalu Park is prized for its rhododendrons, such as* Rhododendron rugosum, *which are zoned at different altitudes up the mountain.*

Opposite, right: *In the montane forest, the trees are gnarled and there is a profusion of mosses and epiphytes that thrive in the damp conditions.*

Above, right: *The dramatic profile of Gunung Kinabalu is characterized by the Donkey's Ears, two granite pinnacles.*

Rich Flora

Kinabalu Park has one of the greatest concentrations of plant species on earth, largely because of the mountain which provides such a range of habitats at different altitudes. It is estimated that over 4,500 species occur here, including about 1,500 orchids, of which 77 are endemic to the park. There are more species of rhododendrons and pitcher plants here than in any similar-sized area. The Rajah Pitcher Plant has the biggest known pitcher of any, up to 2 litres (3½ pints) in capacity, while one of the most elegant is the flask-shaped Low's Pitcher Plant.

Mixed dipterocarp forest dominates most lowland areas and is extremely rich in tree species. From 1,200 metres (4,000 feet) up to 2,350 metres (7,700 feet), lower montane forest grows. Species of oaks, laurels, myrtles, conifers and members of the tea family are among the commoner trees. Higher still, upper montane forest reaches 3,000 metres (9,800 feet), characterized on Gunung Kinabalu by magnificent rhododendrons. Increasingly with altitude the forest becomes moss-covered, gnarled and stunted, until the tree line is reached between 3,350 metres (11,000 feet) and 3,700 metres (12,100 feet). The highest vegetation of all is known as subalpine vegetation, and Gunung Kinabalu is the only Malaysian mountain high enough to support it. Above this, there is no soil on the steep, smooth rocks.

Animal Life

Kinabalu Park's animal life is as outstanding as its flora and includes 289 species of birds, with specialities like

Location: 60 km (37 miles) northeast of Kota Kinabalu.

Climate: Ranging from hot and humid in the lowlands, around 28°C (82°F), to very cold at the summit of Gunung Kinabalu, around 6°–8°C (42°–46°F).

When to Go: Any time of year, perhaps best in March, with usually clear skies and little rain. If possible avoid wetter months around November–February.

Access: Bus or taxi from Kota Kinabalu in about 2 hours; the new Mesilau visitor centre is 5 km (3 miles) further on. About another 1 hour to the lowlands visitor centre at Poring.

Permits: Not required except for climbing Gunung Kinabalu. Small charge for vehicle access.

Equipment: In the lowlands and headquarters, light forest wear and walking boots, with a pullover or jacket in evening. Mountain climbers should take waterproof jacket, warm clothing.

Facilities: Information centre, bookshop, restaurants, accommodation; book well in advance, through Sabah Parks office in Kota Kinabalu. There are various trails near headquarters. On the mountain, a single trail to summit, rest stops, overnight accommodation and restaurant at Panar Laban at 3,300 m (10,850 ft). At Poring, hot springs, baths; canopy walkway.

Watching Wildlife: Magnificent birdwatching opportunities. For botanists, a vast array of plants with many endemics.

Visitor Activities: Birdwatching, walking forest trails, plantwatching. Climbing the peak (about 10% of park visitors do so); usually splendid photo opportunities.

Above: *At lowland Poring, hot spring baths are popular with weekend visitors.*

the Kinabalu Serpent-eagle and Kinabalu Friendly Warbler, Crimson-breasted Wood Partridge and Bornean Mountain Whistler. Not many are confined to Gunung Kinabalu, but they are particularly easy to see in the environment provided around the park head-quarters. There are at least 290 species of butterflies, 100 species of reptiles, 40 species of freshwater fish, and an unknown but vast assemblage of inverte-brates still being studied.

Trekking and Climbing

Around the headquarters at 1,500 metres (5,000 feet) there are several forest trails to explore. There are three mountain ascent routes: the Summit Trail is the one used by all ordinary visitors and tourists, while Kotal's Trail and Bowen's Trail require special permission and, for the latter, rock-climbing experience. Never forget the potential dangers on the mountain.

The trek to Low's Peak takes two days, beginning with an uphill climb all the way to Panar Laban at 3,300 metres (11,000 feet) where there is overnight accommo-dation. Most climbers begin the final ascent at 3 am the next morning, in order to reach the peak at sunrise. The vast landscapes over lowland Sabah, with the sight of the mountain's shadow edging across the clouds, are an indescribable experience. It is then possible to climb all the way down to park head-quarters on the same day.

Poring Hot Springs lie 43 kilome-tres (27 miles) to the southeast. There are five hot springs with bathing facilities, several forest trails leading to waterfalls and caves, and a canopy walk-way. Near the foot of the walkway, *Rafflesia* is sometimes in flower. The walkway itself is good for birdwatching, looking for canopy insects, and viewing the crowns of the biggest trees.

Low's Peak
Oyayubi Iwu Peak ▲   ▲ Ugly Sister King Edward Peak
Peak   ▲
St.Johns Peak ▲   ▲ Donkey Ears Peak
▲ Tunku Abdul
South Peak   Rahman
▲
Sayat-Sayat hut ⌂
Panar Laban hut ⌂
Laban Rata hut ⌂
⌂ Paka cave shelter
Kota Kinabalu
⌂ Villosa shelter
⌂ Layang-Layang hut
Kamborongon   ⌂ Mempening shelter
Telecom Station ● ⌂ Lowii shelter
⌂ Ubah shelter   N
Kandi shelter ⌂
Park HQ □ □ Timpohon Gate

Right: *Geometrid moths include some day-flying forms which have spectacular colouring.*

Far right: *One of Borneo's 33 endemic birds is the spectacular but rarely seen Whitehead's Trogon.*

Right and far right: *Kinabalu is famous for its orchids; some 1,500 species occur here.* Renanthera bella (right) *grows only where the soil is mineral rich.* Bulbophyllum lobbii (far right), *a small orchid species, grows close to ground level.*

Achievements at Kinabalu Park

Kinabalu is an important research site, currently conducting a major study on ethnobotany. There is a montane plant garden which doubles as an exhibit and an opportunity for study. The park also has laboratories, a herbarium, a museum collection and, at headquarters, educational facilities for visitors.

Surrounding the park are areas cultivated by Kadazan Dusun peoples, Sabah's largest community of indigenous residents. Many members of the local community work in the park as rangers and guides, so that the park is able to bring an economic benefit to the surrounding villages. Further benefits flow from the sale of foodstuffs, especially fruit and vegetables, and opportunities to work in the increasing number of hotels.

Right: *Steps help along some stretches of the invariably steep and long ascent of Gunung Kinabalu.*

Below: *One of the most oddly shaped pitcher plants is* Nepenthes lowii, *which grows at mid-mountain altitudes.*

Above, top: *St John's Peak on Gunung Kinabalu shows clear evidence of glacial action in the geological past.*

Above, centre: *An early morning climb to the peak allows plenty of time for a careful descent, following the safety ropes, before the sun gets too hot.*

Above, bottom: *Gunung Kinabalu's massive summit scenery forms a great contrast with the richly forested lowlands below; up here even lichens are scarce.*

Right: *Seen from the agricultural area of Kundasan, Gunung Kinabalu dominates the skyline.*

TURTLE ISLANDS PARK

Turtle Watching in the Sulu Sea

In the shallow waters of the Sulu Sea there is a cluster of small, low, sandy islands which are the nesting sites of a wide-ranging population of Green and Hawksbill Turtles. Three of the islands lie within Malaysia and the remainder in the Philippines. Turtle Islands Park, situated on the Malaysian side of this area, covers an area of 17 square kilometres (6½ square miles), consisting of the tiny islands of Selingaan, Bakkungaan Kecil and Gulisaan, and the adjacent sea and coral reefs. This protected area, established in 1977, is managed by the Sabah Parks authority, whose staff are resident on all three islands to safeguard the park.

Nesting Turtles

The special feature of the park is that two species of turtles come ashore, at night, throughout the year to lay their eggs. The majority are Green Turtles, which lay their eggs between July and October, and favour Selingaan as a nesting site. The remainder are Hawksbills, which lay their eggs between February and April and prefer to nest on Gulisaan where the type of beach and vegetation are particularly favourable and where they can feed on the invertebrate animals of the surrounding coral reefs. The diet of adult Green Turtles consists mainly of marine plants in the shallow waters of open seas. Smaller numbers of both species come to Bakkungaan Kecil.

Opposite: Green Turtles are protected both within the park and by a joint agreement between Malaysia and the Philippines, a first for the region.

Above, right: Colourful marine life, including this starfish, is abundant around the park's coral reefs.

The turtles drag themselves up the beach to a site above high tide and, using their rear flippers, excavate a hole into which the eggs are laid. The eggs are white and spherical and the shell has the texture of thin, tough leather. Green Turtles lay an average of 110 eggs per nest hole, while Hawksbills may lay between about 70 and 200 eggs. After laying, the hole is refilled with sand, again using flippers, and the turtle returns to sea. The whole process takes about one hour. The eggs incubate under the warm sand for 50 to 60 days; their temperature affects the sex of the embryos, with higher temperatures resulting in more females. The baby turtles normally emerge at night and they immediately scramble towards the sea to begin their life swimming and feeding throughout the seas of the Malaysian, Philippine and Indonesian region. It is believed that Green Turtles take at least 30 years to mature before returning to breed.

Turtle Protection

In the late 1960s, nearly 700,000 eggs were laid annually on the turtle islands. Despite protective measures introduced then, egg numbers declined steadily and in 1987 only 223,897 were counted. But in 1988, the number of eggs laid increased significantly for the first time, to 336,475. It is to be hoped that three decades of protection have had permanent positive results.

On the Turtle Islands, the Parks authorities practise a system of digging up eggs as soon as the mother turtle has finished the laying process. The eggs are transferred to a hatchery on the island, where they are replanted at a similar depth. When the hatchlings emerge, they are collected into a bucket and released on the beach. Since

Location: 12 km (7½ miles) off the tip of the Sandakan Peninsula, and 36 km (22 miles) from Sandakan town, eastern Sabah.

Climate: Usually hot and sunny by day, with wetter weather and rougher sea conditions usually from October–February.

When to Go: Turtles nest in every month, most commonly from about July–October when seas are calmer.

Access: By boat from Sandakan harbour; takes about 1 hour by speedboat.

Permits: Obtained from Sabah Parks office in Sandakan town. Accommodation must be booked well in advance.

Equipment: Light clothing which provides protection from the sun. Sunblock cream essential, especially during boat trips when breeze is misleadingly cool. A torch (do not shine this or camera flashlamps at turtles). Swimming and snorkelling or diving gear at the visitor's discretion.

Facilities: On Pulau Selingaan, limited overnight accommodation, an exhibition, restaurant. No public boat service; visitors must make their own arrangements.

Watching Wildlife: Mainly Green and Hawksbill Turtles, by night; also fruit bats, a few birds, and wild plants such as strangling figs, rare yellow-flowered seaside legume Sophora, and *mengkudu* with its foul-smelling fruit.

Visitor Activities: Turtle watching and observing hatchery procedures, usually done at night; swimming, snorkelling, scuba diving, picnicking and general relaxation.

Right: *Green Turtle eggs, reburied and enclosed for collecting and counting, are part of the major effort undertaken throughout the year to ensure that maximum numbers of hatchlings are produced and returned to the sea in safety.*

Below: *The young turtle is most vulnerable during its first few days of life.*

the early 1970s, an average of over 200,000 hatchlings have been released into the sea annually. Only a very small percentage of these reach maturity. Tagging, using metal tags, of some of the adult turtles coming to nest has shown that the turtles may travel into waters of the Philippines and also Indonesia but, most importantly, that the very same turtles return every few years to lay their eggs on the turtle islands, in both Malaysian and Philippine waters.

Visiting the Islands

Sea turtles are the main but not the only attractions of the Turtle Islands. The clear turquoise-coloured sea and

coral reefs are inviting for swimming, snorkelling or scuba diving. Seasonally, when the trees on the islands are in fruit, another interesting nocturnal animal visitor to the park is the Island Flying Fox. These huge bats range over wide areas, moving from island to island wherever they can detect the odour of the ripe fruits on which they feed.

There are limited facilities and accommodation on Selingaan but, because of restrictions on numbers, not everyone who wishes to stay on the island can do so. A larger island, Libaran, situated between Sandakan town and the Turtle Islands Park, represents another chance to see the turtles, though far fewer nest here, presumably because people have occupied the island for a long time, and neither turtles nor their eggs have enjoyed

intensive protection. It is hoped that, with careful planning and management in collaboration with the Philippine authorities, more islands used by turtles on the Philippine side of the border can be made accessible to visitors from Sabah. This will set an unusual precedent for transboundary tourism and conservation.

Top right: As dusk creeps over Pulau Selingaan, the sand awaits the visiting turtles; this is the preferred Green Turtle beach and turtle tracks can be seen here

Centre right: Hawksbill Turtles can be seen around the islands, and nest predominantly on Pulau Gulisaan.

Bottom right: A female Green Turtle excavates a hole in which to lay her eggs.

KABILI-SEPILOK FOREST RESERVE

Orang-utan Rehabilitation in the Forest

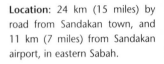

The Kabili-Sepilok Forest Reserve is one of the most important surviving remnants of Sabah's once rich and extensive forested areas. Occupying an area of 43 square kilometres (16 square miles), the reserve is covered almost entirely by lowland forests in which timber trees of the family Dipterocarpaceae predominate both in numbers and in size.

Orang-utans

The Orang-utan Rehabilitation Centre is by far the best known facility in Sepilok and the work here has attracted much attention world wide. The centre was established in 1964 by the Sabah Wildlife Department (at that time a part of the Forestry Department), and aimed to facilitate the rehabilitation of Orang-utans confiscated from

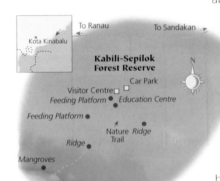

Opposite, top left: *Health is an important criterion in judging whether a rehabilitant Orang-utan is ready to take its first steps into the forest.*

Opposite, centre left: *The long-term programme at Kabili-Sepilok has permitted the monitoring of individual Orang-utans over long periods.*

Opposite, bottom left: *Like any infants, Orang-utans benefit from care and attention while learning how to cope with their environment.*

Opposite, right: *The mixed dipterocarp forest at Kabili-Sepilok is rich in species and provides structural complexity for the animals to move within.*

Above, right: *Massive adult male Orang-utans typically stay at ground level.*

captivity or displaced by forest clearance. Visitors are allowed to interact with the Orang-utans at feeding times, which occur twice a day. The animals are viewed at specially built feeding platforms from boardwalks above the forest floor, so as to minimize the impact of visitor numbers.

The Mangrove Trail

Although most visitors to Sepilok do not venture away from the boardwalks, there are several forest trails that are worth exploring. One of the most accessible is the mangrove trail, which runs from the Rehabilitation Centre and leads over sandstone ridges into the mangrove forests on the boundary of the reserve. Here, a small reception centre has been set up, with basic accommodation facilities.

The trail begins in the low-lying area of the reserve, where flat land supports forests that are seasonally flooded by rain and the floodwater from nearby streams. Here, the Borneo Ironwood is found. These large timber trees, sought after for centuries for their durable wood, are found only in Borneo and the Philippines, and today very few examples exist outside forest reserves. Another rare plant is a small terrestrial orchid, *Cymbidium borneense*, known only from the reserve.

Leading away from the flat ground, the trail begins to ascend the sandstone ridges which dominate the reserve. Different tree species make up the forest here, with large canopy trees such as *Parashorea tomentella* which are common in the lowlands being replaced by *Shorea multiflora* and *Dipterocarpus acutangulus*. This is the hardest part of the trail, leading across the undulating hills, but the air here is not so densely humid as in the lower lying areas of the reserve.

Location: 24 km (15 miles) by road from Sandakan town, and 11 km (7 miles) from Sandakan airport, in eastern Sabah.

Climate: Usually warm by day inside the forest, hotter out in the open, with more likelihood of rain in the afternoon and evening. Wetter weather is more likely from October– February.

When to Go: Any time of year. The centre is open from 9 am–4 pm daily; Orang-utans usually fed about 9.30 or 10 am and 2.30 pm.

Access: By bus, four times daily from Sandakan bus station, or by taxi. You can arrange with a taxi driver for your return.

Permits: Not needed in advance; there is an entrance charge for visitors. If you intend to walk the mangrove trail or visit by boat, permission is required from Sabah Forestry Department which is close to Sepilok outside Sandakan.

Equipment: Ordinary light clothing and footwear, unless you intend to walk along forest trails when stronger boots are useful.

Facilities: Reception area, restaurant, exhibits, trails, boardwalk to the Orang-utan feeding area. Overnight accommodation in various hotels in Sandakan town.

Watching Wildlife: Mainly Orang-utans, but 277 species of birds have been recorded, and there is a range of other lowland forest animals and plants.

Visitor Activities: Orang-utan watching and photography. Do not feed the animals and do not carry food with you. Trail walking. Boat trips to the mangroves.

Right: *Carefully designed boardwalks reduce visitor impact upon the forest, while allowing close and detailed views of plant and animal life.*

Above: *Troops of Pig-tailed Macaques clear up scraps from the feeding platform after the rehabilitant Orang-utans have had their fill in the morning.*

On the descent, the lofty forest begins to lose its stature as it leads into first the fringes and then the main expanse of the mangrove swamp, where the trees grow in deep mud and need specialized roots both to anchor and to breathe. Proboscis Monkeys occur here, and feed almost entirely on the mangrove foliage. The trail ends at the reception centre of Sepilok Laut.

Another way to visit the mangroves is by speedboat from Sandakan. Yet another alternative is to come into the mangroves by boat, and walk out along the trail over the ridges.

Forest Resources

About 2 kilometres (1½ miles) away from the Rehabilitation Centre the Rainforest Interpretation Centre is well worth a visit. From here, a short well-labelled nature trail runs through the arboretum belonging to the Forest Research Centre. Information boards have been erected at selected points to highlight various features of the vegetation.

Specialists who visit Sepilok are still discovering new plant species among its botanical wealth. Recently, a local botanist discovered two new species of palms that can be found only within the reserve. The forest plants also have the potential to supply new drugs and medicines. As a source of seed material for the enrichment of other forested areas, or for the development of forest plantations, the reserve remains a living gene bank of resources. It is also of special interest as a place where inland forest remains continuous down to the coast.

SUNGAI KINABATANGAN

Along Sabah's Longest River

The Kinabatangan Wildlife Sanctuary lies within the vast floodplain of the Sungai Kinabatangan – one of the longest rivers in Malaysia. At 270 square kilometres (104 square miles), the sanctuary is part of an important network of conservation areas in the lowlands of eastern Sabah, together forming a corridor of natural vegetation which links the lower, tidal, mangrove-fringed reaches of the river to the seemingly limitless inland forests of the upper catchment area and its hills.

Lowland Diversity

The Sungai Kinabatangan begins its course deep in the forested interior of Sabah. Where the river reaches the lowlands, a rich mosaic of forests, swamps and limestone outcrops covers one of Malaysia's largest floodplains. In areas where the land remains under water for long periods, the forests give way to open woodlands or to herbaceous swamps that are sometimes almost entirely carpeted with sedges and grasses. Oxbow lakes, formed by large meanders of the river that have been cut off from the main channel, are a common feature.

It is not surprising, given these varied habitats, that there is a bewildering abundance and diversity of wildlife. Among the primates that share the forest are Orang-utans, and during the drier months of the year Asian Elephants, one of the region's most highly endangered species, roam here on their annual migration to the floodplain. In the network of rivers, swamps and lakes many aquatic animals can be found including bony fish, freshwater rays and sharks, and crocodiles. A recent study of the sharks re-discovered a freshwater species not seen during the previous eight decades.

A River Safari

The best way to experience the beauty of Sungai Kinabatangan is by river safari. Village boats, or tourist boats operated by established companies, are available to visitors at some of the riverside villages such as Sukau and Batu Putih. The most magical moments are at dawn, when the chorus of birds and the bubbling calls of the gibbons give a very clear impression of the forest waking up for the day ahead. Often one can hear the unmistakable sound of hornbills in flight, their stiff wing feathers sighing at every beat. Sometimes the more enigmatic of Kinabatangan's inhabitants can be glimpsed: otters at play, or Orang-utans moving slowly and languidly through the forest.

At dusk, Proboscis Monkeys begin to gather along the riverine forest margins. These charismatic primates – the males distinguished by their huge, pendulous red noses – seem relatively undisturbed by humans when they begin to settle to sleep, and are fascinating to watch at close quarters in the fading light.

The Gomantong Caves

The Gomantong Caves lie about 10 kilometres (6 miles) from the visitor lodges at Sukau, and are easily accessible by road. They are within a forest reserve and therefore managed by the Forest Department, though day to day management also relies on the Sabah Wildlife Department because these caves are famous for their swiftlets and bird's nest collecting. In other caves, collectors climb long poles from the ground to reach the nests.

Above, right. A serene atmosphere prevails as evening falls over the impressive Sungai Kinabatangan.

Location: A huge river whose basin occupies much of eastern Sabah, with the estuary on the northern side of Dent Peninsula.

Climate: In the lowland areas hot and humid by day, pleasantly cool by night. Rainy weather more likely in the period from October–February, when there is consequent flooding of some forested areas.

When to Go: Any season, but access is more difficult in wet weather.

Access: By road (preferably 4-wheel drive) from Sandakan, circuitously west then south then east to Gomantong Caves, to reach the commonest access point at Sukau. Sukau is about 32 km (20 miles) from the estuary, and some tour companies prefer to take clients from Sandakan by boat along the coast and upriver.

Permits: Not currently required.

Equipment: Light clothing for boat journeys and forest walking, with strong footwear that can survive frequent wetting. Torch for visiting caves and for night walks.

Facilities: Several private companies operate tourist lodges at Sukau, with full board and lodging, boat services, and can arrange side trips to oxbow lakes and Gomantong Caves.

Watching Wildlife: Proboscis Monkeys and other primates, lowland birds, hornbills, and raptors. A few lucky visitors may see elephants.

Visitor Activities: Watching wildlife, river trips, forest walks, visits to oxbow lakes and caves. Evening boat trip is best to see Proboscis Monkeys (preferably patronize operators using silent electric motors). Look out for Oriental Darter and Storm's Stork.

in the roof but at Gomantong the method is different – from the village on top of the limestone outcrop the collectors descend to the cave through potholes. The price of edible nests is tremendous, reaching several thousand dollars per kilogram, which encourages the collectors to take risks.

Visitors to the caves will become immediately aware of a very strong smell of ammonia which emanates from the vast amount of guano deposited by both swiftlets and bats. This guano, rich in nutrients, is in itself a micro-habitat for millions of invertebrates. The whole mass seethes with cockroaches and crickets.

Towards dusk, troops of Proboscis Monkeys (below) *begin to gather in riverside trees to prepare for sleep. This is often the best time to observe Borneo's most distinctive monkey. Approaching by boat* (below, left), *will afford the closest and most rewarding encounter. The best known site in the area for Proboscis Monkey watching is the Sungai Menanggul* (left), *a tributary of the Kinabatangan.*

Conservation of the Floodplain

Since the early days of trade in Borneo, the Kinabatangan has been one of the major routes for access to the natural resources of the forest: rattans and resins from the trees, and edible birds' nests from the Gomantong Caves have been a few of the valued harvests of the area. The region also provides a constant supply of fresh water and a bounty of fish. Where such resources were near at hand, the Orang Sungai (a broad term applied to the people who settled along the rivers) established their small communities, and over centuries both forest and river have been central to their livelihood. Today, efforts are under way to encourage villagers' participation in tourism.

Working to maintain the balance between the wise use and protection of the floodplain has been the aim of conservation efforts. A partnership will have to be forged that not only includes government and the private sector but also the local people, on whom any developments will have a large impact.

Left and above: *An innovative ladder system enables nest collectors at the Gomantong Caves to harvest swiftlet nests from the cave roof. The much sought-after edible nests are then sorted on the communal verandah.*

Below: *Upriver from where most of the visitor accommodation is located, there is access to a series of oxbow lakes, where crocodiles are known.*

TABIN WILDLIFE RESERVE

A Haven for Large Mammals

Tabin Wildlife Reserve was gazetted in 1984, mainly to protect populations of three endangered large mammal species: Asian Elephants, Sumatran Rhinoceros and Banteng, the Asian wild cattle. A huge rectangle of 1,205 square kilometres (465 square miles), the reserve consists mainly of old logged forest, with several patches of undisturbed forest making up a core area. The land is generally hilly in the centre and west, and flatter to the north where small areas of swamp forest and mangrove can be found near the tributaries of the lower Sungai Segama.

Elephants and Rhinos

The elephant population at Tabin is one of the healthiest in number in Sabah: a 1992 survey estimated that there were somewhere between 212 and 297 animals in the reserve during the dry season. They mostly use the areas of level ground, near rivers, where food plants such as gingers, bananas and bamboo are abundant, and where there is minimal human activity.

Opposite: Within Borneo, Asian Elephants are confined to the eastern part of Sabah; at Tabin they are especially abundant. Consequently, visitors to the reserve can expect good sightings on most visits. Found mainly in the vicinity of the area's rivers, they can often be seen bathing or play fully splashing in the water. An elephant translocation unit has been set up at Tabin to translocate animals from areas where there might be potential conflicts with agriculture.

Above, right: Sun Bears have poor eyesight and can be aggressive if startled at close quarters.

Little is known about the Sumatran Rhinoceros, but in Tabin, surveys during the early 1980s estimated between 7 and 20 individuals, concentrated mainly in the centre of the reserve. Recent records, based on the finding of footprints, are mostly of adults and the long-term viability of the population is uncertain. The rhinos avoid human activities, but are adaptable enough in their diet to move back into logged forest if it is sufficiently undisturbed, and feed on plants amongst the regrowth.

A factor important to elephants, rhinos and other big mammals is the availability of minerals at Tabin, from salt licks, mineral water springs, such as the Tagas-Tagas spring, and mud volcanoes.

Lipad Mud Volcano

Tabin contains three mud volcanoes, the biggest, at Lipad, being easily accessible to visitors along a 2-kilometre (1¼-mile) trail. The route is fairly gentle, with possible sightings of Plantain Squirrel, Plain Pygmy Squirrel and Large Tree-shrew on the way. The volcano covers about 2 hectares (5 acres) and is devoid of vegetation. The active 'cone' is 2 to 3 metres (6 feet) high and consists of bubbling, salty, greyish mud, flowing from sources deep under the ground and particularly rich in sodium and calcium. Footprints of mammals that visit the volcano are always present. Elephants, Sambar Deer, Bearded Pigs, smaller mammals, and even birds come to drink, wallow or lick the mud according to preference.

Research at Tabin

Tabin is particularly interesting to researchers because it is big enough to support viable populations of many ani-

Location: About 50 km (31 miles) northeast of Lahad Datu, in the centre of the Dent Peninsula in eastern Sabah.

Climate: Warm and humid throughout the year. Rainfall heaviest October–February; drier in May and June.

When to Go: Any time of year, but access will be more difficult in wet weather.

Access: By 4-wheel drive vehicle. From Lahad Datu 20 km (12 miles) towards Tungku, then north onto Jalan Porim (earth road) for 17 km (11 miles) to the gate. It is another 9 km (6 miles) to the reserve headquarters.

Permits: Tabin is a research and conservation area, but is open for controlled visits. Permission should be sought well in advance from Sabah Wildlife Department headquarters, Kota Kinabalu, or their district office in Lahad Datu. Permission may be obtained from the reserve manager for special visitors to use the rest house.

Equipment: Visitors should take food and cooking equipment, light clothing, strong walking shoes or boots, compass, binoculars and camera.

Facilities: Headquarters in the Sungai Lipad valley with reception centre, rest house, research lodge and interpretative display. No overnight accommodation.

Watching Wildlife: Most easily done from the earth roads in or adjacent to the reserve; caution and discretion are needed in the face of possible meetings with large mammals.

Visitor Activities: Jungle trekking to mud volcano at Lipad or boulder-caves along river; mammal watching, birdwatching, and associated opportunities for photography and study. Spotlighting to observe nocturnal mammals.

Above: *Mud wallows at Tabin are attractive to big mammals, including the Sumatran Rhinoceros.*

Right: *Individuals within a group of Hose's or Grey Leaf-monkeys can sometimes be distinguished by their face markings.*

Below: *The research quarters at Tabin are an important centre for conservation-related studies.*

mals. Sun Bears, Clouded Leopards, mousedeer, Barking Deer, Grey Leaf-monkeys and Maroon Leaf-monkeys are some of the mammals that occur throughout the reserve. Recent research conducted here has looked at the ecology of civets and jungle cats, as well as that of the rats which form a large part of their diet. This has shown how important it is to retain forest areas near agriculture, because natural predators such as the wild cats live in the forest and help to reduce pests in the adjacent crops. Possibly, the forest can act as a reservoir for other useful species such as owls.

Tabin, as a reasonably large block of forest, albeit somewhat disturbed, is also important as a reservoir for biological diversity in general. Most of the reserve consists of lowland dipterocarp forest, with trees such as *Parashorea tomentella* and *Dipterocarpus caudiferus*. The plant list exceeds 700 species, and there is no doubt that further surveys could push the total recorded to well over 1,000.

DANUM VALLEY CONSERVATION AREA

Research in a Unique Reserve

In 1976 a scientific expedition, sponsored by the Sabah National Parks Board (as it was then named) and funded by WWF Malaysia, was carried out in the Danum area. Based on the diversity of wild species and forest types described, the expedition report recommended that Danum Valley be established as a national park. By then, however, the entire area had been included in a 100-year logging concession of the Sabah Foundation. A statewide faunal survey conducted a few years later concluded that Danum Valley represented one of the most important areas in Sabah for conservation of wild mammals and birds. In 1980, the Foundation decided to retain Danum Valley as a conservation area, on a voluntary basis, within its concession. In 1995, the status of the area was strengthened by converting it into a Protection Forest Reserve, in which no logging is permitted by law.

The Danum Valley Protection Forest Reserve, covering 438 square kilometres (169 square miles), is a part of the upper catchment area of the Sungai Segama. Surrounded by vast timber production forests, Danum Valley is protected by a wide buffer zone of natural forests on all sides, ensuring that breeding populations of rare animals can be sustained.

Plants and Animals

About 1,300 species of plants have been recorded here. Amongst those of interest are two dipterocarps, *Parashorea malaanonan* and *P. tomentella* (probably the most abundant large trees in the natural forests of this part of Sabah); *Citrus macroptera* (a wild tree with large yellow fruits); *Mangifera pajang* (a large tree of the mango family); and *Nenga gajah* (a very rare palm, known only from Danum Valley and the island of Sumatra, Indonesia). On the mountains within Danum Valley are several species of native coniferous trees, four species of pitcher plants, a rare slipper orchid and a climbing or scrambling bamboo.

Animal life is also impressive. Studies to date have recorded 124 species of mammals, 275 species of birds, 72 species of reptiles, 56 species of amphibians and 37 species of fish. The mammals include 10 species of primates (among them Orang-utan and Red Leaf-monkey), Asian Elephant, Sumatran Rhinoceros, Banteng (a species of wild cattle), Sun Bear and Clouded Leopard. All the species of hornbills known to occur in Borneo have been recorded at Danum Valley, and there are seven species of pitta, colourful yet secretive birds of shady, damp parts of the forest floor.

Visiting the Area

Four fifths of the Danum Valley area is hilly, with a high point of 1,090 metres (3,585 feet) at the peak of Gunung Danum. The steepness of this terrain and the difficulty of navigating the rivers that pass through it mean that most visitor activities are confined to the lower lying land. Adventurous trekkers may be able to reach some of the imaginatively named remoter areas

Above, right: Crimson Sunbirds are among the brilliantly coloured birds of the forest edge.

Location: In southeastern Sabah, in forested country about 70 km (44 miles) west of Lahad Datu.

Climate: Hot and humid by day, equable within the forest by night. Like many forested areas in Borneo, frequently wet, with more rain likely between September and February.

When to Go: Any time of year.

Access: Borneo Rainforest Lodge is reached by a 2½ hour drive from Lahad Datu town, on a gravel road through regenerating logged forests.

Permits: Not required to visit the Borneo Rainforest Lodge, but those wishing to stay at the research centre or to undertake research must obtain permission through one of the participating organizations, usually with a local collaborator.

Equipment: Light clothing, leech socks, sturdy shoes or boots, insect repellant are all useful.

Facilities: Borneo Rainforest Lodge offers nature interpretation trails, a canopy walkway, night-time wildlife viewing, and arranges events where visitors can see Danum Valley research.

Watching Wildlife: A broad array of lowland forest species, many of them rare elsewhere. Big mammals are seldom seen, but elephants may be heard. Orang-utans, gibbons, other primates, including tarsier at night.

Visitor Activities: Mainly bird-watching, animal watching, botanizing and general nature study in the forest. Swimming in cool rivers near Borneo Rainforest Lodge. Viewing forest regeneration programmes, replanting trials, reduced impact logging research. Slide and video presentation by trained naturalists.

Above: *The curiously flat-tened File-eared Treefrog, found only in Borneo, delivers its ratchet-like call by night.*

Above, right: *The Oriental Dwarf Kingfisher's diet includes frogs and insects found far from rivers.*

Right: *A Scarlet-rumped Trogon typically sits quietly, peering around for big insects.*

Far right: *Of eight species of hornbills found here, the most rarely encountered is the White-crowned Hornbill.*

Far right, below: *The Red-bearded Bee-eater is found in the middle and upper levels of the forest.*

Opposite: *The canopy walkway provides superb opportunities to compare life at treetop level with that near the ground.*

such as Dismal Gorge, where there are falls and rapids, or Mount Tribulation which, though not very high, is par-ticularly steep and has interesting vegetation rich in ferns, orchids and pitcher plants.

In 1994, the Borneo Rainforest Lodge, situated on the banks of the Sungai Danum, about 10 kilometres (6 miles) from the Field Centre, was opened to cater for tourists. There are several good swimming places found close to the Lodge and visitor trails extend from here through varied forest, some of it selectively logged and much of it undisturbed, at the margin of the Danum Valley. Trekkers can take self-guided walks along a marked trail system, or arrange to be accompanied by a guide or experienced naturalist. A canopy walkway suspended more than 25 metres (80 feet) above the forest floor allows one to get closer views of the plant and ani-mal life at a higher level.

More specialized activities are also available. During a night-time drive by open jeep along one of the trails, it is possible to use a spotlight to look for nocturnal ani-mals. Luck plays a great part in determining what you see: mousedeer are quite common, and various species

of civets, flying squirrels, barking deer and bearded pigs are all possible, though not guaranteed.

Research Projects

An international collaborative research programme has conducted well over 100 studies in the area since 1984. Based at the Danum Valley Field Centre these include comparisons between the plant and animal life of undisturbed and logged forests, and ecological studies of tree-shrews, rhinoceros and mousedeer.

Research projects have also uncovered unexpected human artefacts, such as large jars of Chinese origin and iron-wood coffins, and human bones have been found along the Sungai Danum and upper reaches of the Sungai Segama dating from at least the 17th centu-ry. However, most of Danum Valley appears not to have suffered any human disturbance other than that from occasional hunting parties. Far from detracting from the value of this protected forest, the interesting findings of past human activities show how even remote forests in Borneo may change over long periods.

SIPADAN AND THE SEMPORNA ISLANDS

Malaysia's Premier Dive Sites

The most southwesterly big peninsula in Sabah, the Dent Peninsula, is surrounded by a cluster of islands. The area is remote and wild. Sipadan, a tiny island, has been protected since 1933, but more recent proposals for marine protection are still being refined.

Pulau Sipadan

Pulau Sipadan is Malaysia's only island situated beyond the continental shelf, in oceanic waters, and rises from a depth of over 600 metres (2,000 feet). Extending over 16.4 hectares (40½ acres), it has attractive white sandy beaches but little natural vegetation left: many visitor huts cater for the needs of divers from all over the world. The island's spectacular coral reefs teem with a rich variety of marine life.

From Semporna, the nearest mainland town, a fast boat takes about an hour. The most interesting sight on the way is the occasional water village perched above the coral reefs (though these are not good for the corals).

Opposite, top left: Pulau Sipadan's abundant reef life ranges from large barrel sponges to minute colourful fish.

Opposite, centre left: Bigeye Trevallies are one of several fish species that form large circling shoals.

Opposite, bottom left: Sipadan is outstanding in enabling divers to swim with large numbers of Green Turtles.

Opposite, right: The coral gardens here form part of an underwater paradise that deserves protection forever.

Above, right: The narrow, white-sand shore of Pulau Sipadan is shaded by elegant windswept palms.

Sipadan is the country's premier diving site, and one of the best in the world. The most spectacular sight is the drop-off zone at the edge of the reef, which is characterized by vertical or overhanging rock faces and in some places goes down to 600 metres (2,000 feet). Most of the dive sites have been given names such as Barracuda Point, Coral Gardens, Turtle Patch and Staghorn Crest; all of these are well known snorkelling and diving spots.

The reef rim, which lies just beyond the crest of the reef, is the most actively growing area for corals. The smaller fish to be seen in this part include butterfly-fish, damselfish and groupers. There are also medium-sized to large open water species such as snappers and surgeonfish. Whitetip Reef Sharks, turtles and manta rays visit the area.

One cave in the reef wall acts as a trap for unwary turtles, which occasionally die there; bones or skulls can still be seen. Some turtles still nest on the beaches of Sipadan, and you may be lucky enough to see one of the very few remaining Coconut Crabs. The island has been a bird sanctuary for many years, administered by the Sabah Wildlife Department; apart from Pied Imperial Pigeons and a few other species, a bird to look out for is the White-throated Mangrove Whistler, a Philippine bird with a foothold here in Borneo.

The Semporna Islands

About 50 kilometres (30 miles) to the north is an archipelago of somewhat larger islands, also reached by boat from the town of Semporna, though the trip is more difficult to arrange as tour companies do not specialize in these islands, which include Sebangkat, Selakan, Maiga,

Location: Semporna town is at the tip of the most southeasterly peninsula in Sabah, 350 km (218 miles) from Kota Kinabalu and at the extreme opposite side of the state. The Semporna Islands extend to the north and east while Sipadan and Mabul are to the south.

Climate: Hot, often rather dry.

When to Go: Any time of year; expect calmer seas from March–July, and wetter, rougher conditions from October onwards.

Access: By air or overland to Tawau, thence by bus or taxi to Semporna. Arrange with tour companies prior to your arrival for visits to both Sipadan and Mabul. Travel to the Semporna Islands can be arranged at Semporna jetty.

Permits: Not required, but those visiting the Semporna Islands should inform the police in Semporna town, giving personal and travel details.

Equipment: Make sure boat owners provide life jackets. On Sipadan, tour companies should provide all necessities and rent out diving equipment. Visitors to Semporna Islands must take all necessities including food and means of cooking.

Facilities: Several companies have huts on Sipadan, and dive guides. On the Semporna Islands there are no facilities. On Mabul there are two dive resorts.

Watching Wildlife: Excellent opportunities to see a wide range of fish, corals and invertebrates. Limited range of terrestrial wildlife; including Coconut Crabs.

Visitor Activities: On Sipadan, mainly scuba diving, at a range of sites round the island, by day or at night.

Map labels: Kota Kinabalu / Boat to Semporna / West Ridge / Wildlife Department / Pulau Sipadan / Jetty / Lobster Lairs / Lighthouse / Turtle Cavern/tomb / Barracuda Point / **Sipadan Marine Park** / Staghorn Crest / Coral Gardens / White-tip Avenue / Turtle Patch / N

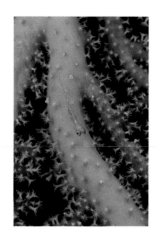

Above: *A camouflaged goby, perched on a fan coral, has an almost transparent body.*

Sibuan, the beautiful Bodgaya, Boheydulang and Tetagan. There is evidence of raised reefs in some areas: Pulau Selangan consists entirely of raised reef limestone, and the town of Semporna is built on an old coral reef, estimated to be around 35,000 years old. Their exposure is due to a general uplifting of the land and surrounding sea bed. Other islands are of volcanic origin. Both Pulau Bodgaya and Boheydulang represent the northern rim of a now flooded and extinct volcanic caldera with the southern rim completely submerged.

Approaching the central islands of Bodgaya, Boheydulang and Tetagan, you will be captivated by the emerald green lagoon sheltered by the surrounding steep cliffs of these three islands. The lagoon is about 8 kilometres (5 miles) across, and the cliffs reach up to 460 metres (1,500 feet) above the sea. The coral reefs here are less colourful than in Sipadan, but may contain more variety. The waters around the islands are clear and warm, and the beaches really are white, especially on Pulau Sibuan.

Getting Around

The best way to appreciate the Semporna Islands is to take a cruise, by renting a small village boat. There are no accommodation facilities on any of the islands, though some are inhabited. On Pulau Maiga there is a community of Taosug people, who have built houses from coconut leaves and nipah palm thatch, on stilts at the water's edge. The men and children here fish for food, and some of the villagers build small boats, apparently from driftwood on the shore. There are more

permanent villages on Pulau Boheydulang and Bodgaya. There is some land clearance here, but most of the resident Bajau Samal and Taosug people are fishermen.

The closest island offering any degree of comfort is Pulau Mabul, halfway between Pulau Sipadan and Semporna, where there is a settlement and chalets built on stilts over the water. Alternatively, it is possible to use Semporna town as a base and make day trips.

Right: *The water's astonishing clarity and the variety of reef life make this area a diver's dream.*

Below: *Fantastically branched and brilliantly coloured colonies of sea fans are prolific here.*

Opposite, below: *A yellow pair of Masked Rabbitfish glide past a superb coral garden.*

Overleaf: *Crystal-clear waters and white-sand beaches are characteristic of the idyllic Semporna Islands.*

SUMMARY OF CONSERVATION AREAS

The following is a brief summary of all the conservation areas known to be currently functioning in Peninsular Malaysia, Sarawak and Sabah. Many of them are covered in this book. Some have been established primarily for research and are not generally accessible to tourists. A number of areas proposed as parks by differing authorities have been included in the list; these are at varying stages in the process of creation. When planning a trip, check the 'Visitor Information' panels given for each area described in the book and contact the appropriate authority (see page 174).

Peninsular Malaysia

Belum and Temenggor Forest Reserves (2,000 km^2/772 sq miles). State: Perak. Gazetted 1989. Lake, forests, fruit trees, important for big mammals, monkeys and hornbills.

Bukit Kutu Wildlife Reserve (30 km^2/11^1/$_2$ sq miles) State: Selangor. Gazetted 1922. Hill forest and wildlife. Of both historical and botanical importance.

Cameron Highlands Wildlife Sanctuary (649 km^2/250 sq miles). State: Pahang. Gazetted 1962. Montane forest, tea estates, birds, small mammals, rare and endemic plants.

Endau Rompin National Park (489 km^2/189 sq miles). States: Crosses borders of Pahang and Johor. Gazetted 1989. Montane and riverine habitats, fan-palms. Important for presence of Sumatran Rhinoceros, endemic plants, biogeographic link with Borneo.

Four Islands Bird Reserve (2 ha/5 acres). State: Pahang. Gazetted 1954. Formerly roosting site for seabirds, pigeons. Current situation unknown.

Fraser's Hill Wildlife Reserve (29 km^2/11 sq miles) State: Selangor. Gazetted 1922. Montane forest. Important for birds, flowering plants.

Krau Wildlife Reserve (520 km^2/200 sq miles) State: Pahang. Gazetted 1924. Important for research on Siamang, monkeys, transition from lowland to montane wildlife.

Kuala Selangor Nature Park (324 ha/800 acres). State: Selangor. Gazetted 1989. Coastal habitat, mangroves. Important for migrating waders, otters, leaf-monkeys.

Kuala Selangor Wildlife Reserve (44 ha/108 acres). State: Selangor. Gazetted 1922. Adjoining the Nature Park. Historical site, easy to see leaf-monkeys.

Melaka Islands. State: Melaka. Proposed bird sanctuary for various species of open country and coast.

Mersing Marine Park. State: Johor. Gazetted 1984. Waters surrounding 13 islands. Corals, fish, marine life representative of South China Sea.

Nakawan State Park (50 km^2/20 sq miles). State: Perlis. Proposed. Important for Stump-tailed Macaque, limestone flora and fauna, caves.

Pahang Tua Bird Sanctuary (13 km^2/5 sq miles). State: Pahang. Gazetted 1954. Coastal birdlife.

Port Dickson Islands Bird Sanctuary (2 ha/5 acres). State: Negeri Sembilan. Gazetted 1926. Coastal birdlife.

Pulau Payar Marine Park. State: Kedah. Gazetted 1985. Waters surrounding four islands. Coral reefs and marine life, transitional between Straits of Melaka and Andaman Sea.

Pulau Redang Marine Park. State: Terengganu. Gazetted 1984. Includes waters surrounding nine islands. Coral reefs and associated marine life. Beaches for turtle nesting.

Pulau Tioman Marine Park. State: Pahang. Gazetted 1984. Waters surrounding nine islands. Coral reefs, marine life, including sharks. On Pulau Tioman itself a Wildlife Reserve (72 km^2/28 sq miles) was established in 1972.

Rompin Endau Park (300 km^2/116 sq miles). State: Pahang. Gazetted 1986. Sandstone cliffs in forest, flora with Borneo affinities, birdlife and mammals.

Sungai Dusun Wildlife Reserve (43 km^2/16^1/$_2$ sq miles). State: Selangor. Gazetted 1964. Important for Sumatran Rhinoceros, peat swamp forest, sealing-wax palms.

Sungkai Wildlife Reserve (25 km^2/10 sq miles). State: Perak. Gazetted 1921. Important captive breeding station. Wildlife of lowland and hill forest.

Taman Negara (4,343 km^2/1,680 sq miles). States: Covers adjoining areas of Pahang, Kelantan and Terengganu. Gazetted 1938/39. Malaysia's largest park. Especially important for lowland forests and associated wildlife, many rare plants, Peninsula's highest mountain, caves, very wide range of species in all groups.

Taman Rimba Kenong (130 km^2/50 sq miles). State: Pahang. Gazetted as a forest reserve in 1918, used as a park since 1988. Important for large mammals, central Peninsular flora, limestone caves, excellent lowland forest and undisturbed streams.

Tasik Bera (384 km^2/148 sq miles). State: Pahang. Gazetted 1995. RAMSAR site. Rare natural lake, fish community, peat swamp forest.

Virgin Jungle Reserves

In addition to the areas listed above, the various states in Peninsular Malaysia contain about 80 Virgin Jungle Reserves which are mostly small (less than 10 km^2/4 sq miles) plots of untouched forest within larger blocks of commercial production forest. A proportion of forest on steep land is classified as Protection Forest.

Sarawak

Bako National Park (27 km^2/10 sq miles; extension proposed). Gazetted 1957. Variety of forest types, pitcher plants, Proboscis Monkeys, sandstone formations and forest on sandstone plateau.

Batang Ai National Park (240 km^2/93 sq miles). Gazetted 1991. Important for protection of Orang-utan. Nearby man-made lake. Iban longhouse communities.

Batu Laga Wildlife Sanctuary. Proposed. Wide variety of wildlife characteristic of lowland and hilly forest.

Gunung Gading National Park (41 km^2/16 sq miles). Gazetted 1983. Established for the protection of *Rafflesia* plants.

Gunung Mulu National Park (528 km^2/204 sq miles; extension proposed). Gazetted 1974. Limestone mountains and caves. Very important for species diversity, wildlife and plants in forest over alluvial terraces, wide range of forest types.

Hose Mountains National Park. Proposed. Varied wildlife of hilly forest, up to montane altitudes.

Kubah National Park (22 km^2/8$^1/_2$ sq miles). Gazetted 1989. One of the most important sites in the world for palms.

Lambir Hills National Park (70 km^2/27 sq miles). Gazetted 1973. Important for rain forest research, one of the most diverse tree sites in the world.

Lanjak-Entimau Wildlife Sanctuary (1,688 km^2/652 sq miles; extension proposed). Gazetted 1983. Hill forest. Protects Orang-utans, gibbons and hornbills.

Loagan Bunut National Park (107 km^2/41 sq miles). Gazetted 1991. Rare natural lake surrounded by peat swamp forest.

Maludam Wildlife Sanctuary. Proposed. Peat swamp forest with rare leaf-monkeys and other wildlife.

Niah National Park (31 km^2/12 sq miles). Gazetted 1975. Huge limestone caves with bats and edible birds' nests. Premier archaeological site.

Pelagus National Park. Proposed. River rapids, wildlife in adjacent forest.

Pulau Bruit National Park. Proposed. Mangroves and mudflats, with migrant waders and seabirds.

Pulau Tokong Ara-Banun Wildlife Sanctuary (1.4ha/3$^1/_2$ acres). Feeding and roosting site for various birds.

Pulong Tau National Park. Proposed. High altitude forest and associated wildlife.

Samunsam Wildlife Sanctuary (60 km^2/24 sq miles; extension proposed). Gazetted 1979. Mixed forests. Proboscis Monkeys.

Semengoh Wildlife Rehabilitation Centre (740ha/1,827 acres). Gazetted 1984. Established to rescue captive animals (Orang-utans, monkeys, hornbills) and return them to the wild.

Sibuti Bird Sanctuary. Proposed. Coastal habitat, mangroves and peat swamp.

Similajau National Park (70 km^2/27 sq miles). Gazetted 1976. Coastal forest, beautiful scenery. Coastal and lowland forest animals.

Stutong Nature Reserve (33 ha/81 acres). Gazetted 1994. Coastal vegetation and wildlife.

Talang-Satang Marine Park. Proposed. Nesting turtles, terns, marine life.

Tanjung Datu National Park (14 km^2/5 sq miles). Gazetted 1994. Unusual mixed forest, coastal vegetation, undisturbed streams. Important for birds, nesting turtles.

Usun Apau National Park. Proposed. High altitude forest, hill and montane wildlife.

Wind Cave and Fairy Cave Nature Reserve (115 ha/284 acres). Gazetted 1994. Recreational areas, caves and associated fauna.

Sabah

Crocker Range National Park (1,399 km^2/540 sq miles). Gazetted 1984. Montane forests, *Rafflesia*, diverse bird life.

Danum Valley Conservation Area (438 km^2/169 sq miles). Implemented 1980. Important research area for plants and animals. Undisturbed virgin lowland forest.

Kabili-Sepilok Forest Reserve (43 km^2/16 sq miles). Gazetted 1956. Site of Orang-utan Rehabilitation Centre. Mangrove forests, lowland dipterocarp forest.

Kinabalu Park (754 km^2/291 sq miles). Gazetted 1964. Highest mountain in Southeast Asia. Diverse country from lowland forest to granite peaks. Important for plants (especially orchids). Malaysia's premier bird-watching area.

Kota Belud Bird Sanctuary (120 km^2/46 sq miles). Gazetted 1971. Birds of coasts, open country and ricefields, including herons and egrets.

Kulamba Wildlife Reserve (207 km^2/80 sq miles). Gazetted 1984. Lowland forest with associated flora and fauna, big mammals.

Labuan Marine Park. Federal Territory of Labuan. Gazetted 1994. Waters surrounding islands of Pulau Kuramun, Pulau Rusukan Kecil, Pulau Rusukan Besar. Corals and marine life.

Maliau Basin Conservation Area (390 km^2/150 sq miles). Gazetted 1983. Unusual sandstone ridge, waterfalls, forest.

Pulau Mantanani Bird Sanctuary (about 5 km^2/2 sq miles). Mantanani Scops-owl, other small-island birds, seabirds.

Pulau Tiga Park (158 km^2/61 sq miles). Gazetted 1978. Three small islands and surrounding sea. Noted for sea snakes, mud volcano. Terns and other seabirds offshore.

Sipadan Bird Sanctuary (16.4 ha/40$^1/_2$ acres). Gazetted 1933. Protects Pied Imperial Pigeon, White-throated Mangrove Whistler, among others.

Tabin Wildlife Reserve (1,205 km^2/465 sq miles). Gazetted 1984. Protects Asian Elephant, Sumatran Rhinoceros and Banteng (wild cattle).

Tawau Hills Park (280 km^2/108 sq miles). Gazetted 1979. Broad range of flora and fauna in hilly forest.

Tunku Abdul Rahman Park (50 km^2/20 sq miles). Gazetted 1974. Protects five islands and surrounding waters. Excellent reefs.

Turtle Islands Park (17 km^2/6$^1/_2$ sq miles). Gazetted 1977. Important nesting site for Green and Hawksbill Turtles.

Virgin Jungle Reserves and Protection Forests

Sabah has about 50 Virgin Jungle Reserves, which are mostly small blocks of untouched forest within the commercial production forest, and also some 42 Protection Forests that are set aside by specific legislative enactment.

USEFUL ADDRESSES

The following list includes the authorities responsible for the conservation and management of Malaysia's parks, and a range of other relevant organizations. The information panels for each of the areas covered in this book will tell you who to contact if visitor permits are required.

Peninsular Malaysia

Association of Backpackers Malaysia
No. 6 Jalan SS3/33, 47300 Petaling Jaya

Department of Fisheries Malaysia
Floors 8 & 9, Wisma Tani, Jalan Sultan Salahuddin, 50628 Kuala Lumpur
tel: 03-2982011; fax: 03-2910305; e-mail:hqhelp@dof.mda.my

Department of Wildlife and National Parks
Km. 10, Jalan Cheras, 50664 Kuala Lumpur
tel: 03-9052872; fax: 03-9052873; e-mail: kp@jphltn.sains.my

Forestry Department Headquarters Peninsular Malaysia
Jalan Sultan Salahuddin, 50660 Kuala Lumpur
tel: 03-2988244; fax: 03-2925657; e-mail: uts@forestry.gov.my

Johor Parks Board
JKR 475, Bukit Timbalan, 80000 Johor Bahru
tel: 07-2237471; fax: 07-2237472; e-mail: npcjohor@tm.net.my

Malaysian Nature Society
PO Box 10750, 50724 Kuala Lumpur
tel: 03-6329422; fax: 03-6358773; e-mail: natsoc@po.jaring.my

Malaysian Society of Marine Sciences
PO Box 250, Jalan Sultan PO, 46730 Petaling Jaya
fax: 03-7348065

Malaysia Tourism Promotion Board
Floors 24-27, Menara Dato' Onn, Putra World Trade Centre, 45 Jalan Tun Ismail, 50480 Kuala Lumpur
tel: 03-2935188; fax: 03-2935884

Ministry of Culture, Arts and Tourism
Floors 34-36, Menara Dato' Onn, Putra World Trade Centre, 45 Jalan Tun Ismail, 50694 Kuala Lumpur
tel: 03-2937111; fax: 03-2910951

Wetlands International (Asia Pacific)
Institute of Higher Studies, University of Malaya, 59100 Kuala Lumpur
tel: 03-7572176; fax: 03-7571225; e-mail: wiap@wiap.nasionet.net

World Wide Fund For Nature (WWF) Malaysia
Locked Bag No. 911, Jalan Sultan PO, 46990 Petaling Jaya
tel: 03-7033772; fax: 03-7035157; e-mail: wwfmal@pop.jaring.my

Sarawak

National Parks and Wildlife Office
Sarawak Forestry Department, Wisma Sumber Alam, Jalan Stadium, Petra Jaya, 93660 Kuching
tel: 082-319126; fax: 082-441702

Sarawak Tourism Board
No. 3.43 & 3.44, Level 3, Wisma Satok, Jalan Satok/Kulas, 93400 Kuching
tel: 082-423600; fax: 082-416700; e-mail: sarawak@po.jaring.my

Sabah

Sabah Forest Department
PO Box 311, 90007 Sandakan
tel: 089-660811; fax: 089-669170

Sabah Parks
PO Box 10626, 88806 Kota Kinabalu (street address: Block K, Lot 3, Sinsuran Complex, 88806 Kota Kinabalu)
tel: 088-212508; fax: 088-211585

Sabah Tourism Promotion Corporation
Mail Bag 12, 88999 Kota Kinabalu (street address: 51 Jalan Gaya, 88000 Kota Kinabalu)
tel: 088-218620; fax: 088-212075; e-mail: sabah@po.jaring.my

Sabah Wildlife Department
5th floor, Block B, Wisma MUIS, Sembulan, 88300 Kota Kinabalu (tel: 088-214317; fax: 088-222476; e-mail: jhlsabah@tm.net.my

FURTHER READING

Further reading
Bernard, H.-U. (1991) *Insight Guide: Southeast Asia Wildlife*. APA Publications, Hong Kong.

Bransbury, J. (1993) *A Birdwatcher's Guide to Malaysia*. Waymark Publishing, Australia.

Carcasson, R.H. (1977) *A Field Guide to the Reef Fishes of Tropical Australia and the Indo-Pacific Region*. Collins, London and Sydney.

Corbet, A.S. and Pendlebury, H.N. (1986) *The Butterflies of the Malay Peninsula* (4th edn). Malayan Nature Society, Kuala Lumpur.

Corner, E.J.H. (1988) *Wayside Trees of Malaya* (3rd edn/2 vols). Malayan Nature Society, Kuala Lumpur.

Cox, M.J., van Dijk, P.P., Nabhitabhata, J. and Thirakhupt, K. (1998) *A Photographic Guide to Snakes and Other Reptiles of Peninsular Malaysia, Singapore and Thailand*. New Holland Publishers, London.

Davison, G.W.H. and Chew, Y.F. (1995) *A Photographic Guide to the Birds of Peninsular Malaysia and Singapore*. New Holland Publishers, London.

Davison, G.W.H. and Chew, Y.F. (1996) *A Photographic Guide to the Birds of Borneo*. New Holland Publishers, London.

Henderson, M.R. (1974) *Malayan Wild Flowers* (2 vols). Malayan Nature Society, Kuala Lumpur.

Inger, R.S. and Chin, P.K. (1990) *The Freshwater Fishes of North Borneo* (reprint). Sabah Zoological Society, Kota Kinabalu.

Inger, R.S. and Stuebing, R.B. (1989) *Frogs of Sabah*. Sabah Parks Trustees, Kota Kinabalu.

Inger, R.S. and Tan, F.L. (1996) *The Natural History of Amphibians and Reptiles in Sabah*. Natural History Publications (Borneo), Kota Kinabalu.

Jackson, J. (1995) *The Dive Sites of Malaysia and Singapore*. New Holland Publishers, London.

King, B., Woodcock, M. and Dickinson, E. (1975) *A Field Guide to the Birds of South East Asia*. Collins, London.

Medway, Lord (1981) *The Wild Mammals of Malaya (Peninsular Malaysia) and Singapore* (2nd edn). Oxford University Press, Kuala Lumpur.

Mohsin, A.K.M. and Azmi, A. (1983) *Freshwater Fishes of Peninsular Malaysia*. Universiti Pertanian Malaysia, Serdang.

Moore, W. and Cubitt, G. (1995) *This is Malaysia*. New Holland Publishers, London.

Payne, J. and Cubitt, G. (1990) *Wild Malaysia: The Wildlife and Scenery of Peninsular Malaysia, Sarawak and Sabah*. New Holland Publishers, London.

Payne, J., Cubitt, G and Lau, D. (1994) *This is Borneo*. New Holland Publishers, London.

Payne, J., Francis, C.M. and Phillipps, K. (1985) *A Field Guide to the Mammals of Borneo*. World Wildlife Fund, Kuala Lumpur.

Polunin, I. (1988) *Plants and Flowers of Malaysia*. Times Editions, Singapore.

Smythies, B.E. (1981) *The Birds of Borneo* (3rd edn). Sabah Society and Malayan Nature Society, Kota Kinabalu and Kuala Lumpur.

Strange, M. and Jeyarajasingam, A. (1993) *Birds: A Photographic Guide to the Birds of Peninsular Malaysia and Singapore*. Sun Tree Publications, Singapore.

Tweedie, M.W.F. (1983) *The Snakes of Malaya*. Singapore National Printers, Singapore.

Wells, D. (1998) *The Avifauna of the Malay Peninsula*. Academic Press, London.

Whitmore, T.C. (1977) *The Palms of Malaya*. Oxford University Press, Kuala Lumpur.

Wong, M.P. (1991) *Sipadan: Borneo's Underwater Paradise*. Odyssey Publishing, Singapore.

INDEX